The Tinsmith's Son

by

Joe Werner

authorHOUSE™

1663 LIBERTY DRIVE, SUITE 200
BLOOMINGTON, INDIANA 47403
(800) 839-8640
WWW.AUTHORHOUSE.COM

First published by AuthorHouse 2/14/2006

ISBN: 1-4208-9456-0 (sc)
ISBN: 1-4208-9457-9 (dj)

Library of Congress Control Number: 2005909848

Printed in the United States of America
Bloomington, Indiana

This book is printed on acid-free paper.

Edited By

Lynsey Freeman

The Tinsmith''s Son is the memoir of a boy in Memphis growing into adulthood during the latter part of the depression, How he worked at a tin shop on skid row, ready to go under at any time, and a Dad who fought a constant battle for its survival.

From working on roofs where the pitch would blind and fill the lungs with sulphur, crawling under houses smelling the booze of the man next to him, or the exhilaration he felt as he covered steeples high above the city; it is the story of a lad as he grows to become a man in the sheet metal business. It''s the tale of the tinner''s who drank hard, chased women, did grueling work, but had compassion, kindness, and wisdom.

The Tinsmith''s Son brings to life the rancorous shenanigan''s of these men, and the people of the street. The high-steppers, and the down-and-outer''s who suffered through the depression, but kept their dignity.

From those bittersweet times emerges the story of a boy and girl as they fell in love and the way that love shaped their lives. Through the eyes of these youngster''s passes on to the the reader all the passion, curiosity, and joy as they grew together. Werner brings to life the sadness and anquish of a wife as she deals with the loss of newborn babies, and her grit and determination to have a healthy child. Its a wonderful book of dreams and how those dreams really did come true.

THE TINSMITH'S SON

In Fond Remembrance of

M. Blake Arnoult, M.D.

To My Grandchildren

Amie, Lisa, Patrick, &

Phillip

With All My Love

For everything you have missed, you have gained something else, and for everything you gain, you lose something.

Ralph Waldo Emerson

HARD TIMES

It was an ordinary day for Memphis in July, the heat was brutal and the humidity was thick enough to peel. The boy was fifteen, working with a crew installing copper flashing, nailing it to the wood decking so that it could become part of the finished roof. The only people around were the black roofers, leaning against their mops patiently waiting for the skinny white boy to finish so that they could complete the roof. The copper blistered his hands, and the pitch burned his eyes and took his breath away. As he finished he laid his tools down, leaned his back against the wall and cried without shame, not even trying to hide the tears, and for the first time acknowledged that this was to be his life for the summers to come.

CONTENTS

1

GRANDPA STARTS A TINSHOP

The Depression began in the Northern states in 1929, and quickly spread to the South. By September of 1930, the year of my birth, Memphis, like the rest of the country, was in the worst economic downturn in our nation's history. The Marxist Revolution was five years away, and the Second World War, which was to turn the world into an inferno, would not begin for the United States until 1941. The bad times began in Europe before becoming global and impacting the United States. Although times would be tough, our family had already begun a new life in America.

My dad's parents were of German ancestry, both born in a little town in northern Germany. Fleeing one of Germany's periodic potato famines in the 1800's, the Werner family had immigrated to the United States and somehow settled in New Iberia, Louisiana.

Grandpa quickly saw that an area that grew plants for Tabasco sauce was hardly the place for a tinsmith. After a few years of living in an area populated mainly by Cajun people, with their wonderful unorthodox ways, the family moved to St. Louis and eventually to Memphis where there was a large German population, which created a greater sense of belonging for the family.

The Werner family patriarch, my grandpa, who moved the family to America, was a person of peculiar ways who scared the hell out of us as children. He could be seen, at times, smoking as many as two packs of cigarettes a day and drinking copious amounts of beer from the corner tavern, then not touching anything for weeks. He was a giant man with a voice that roared throughout the old barn of a place on Jones Street with its rattling windows and many rooms where even a whisper could be heard from room to room. He, his wife, and seven children called the place home. Outside, the front yard was shaded by two huge Magnolia trees, which were raided of their blooms weekly by a little gnomelike man. Monk, as he was known, would take the fresh sweet blossoms to sell at the famous Peabody Hotel each week. But whatever the conditions of the house itself or its surroundings, there was always a sense of belonging imparted within.

There were always lots of visitors at Jones Street making the family home a gathering place: the many aunts, uncles, and cousins all milling around the old place, hollering at each other, and squawking away at the same time, sounding like a bunch of geese. I remember it was at these times that Grandpa would give us kids each a nickel to go to the corner grocery for candy and sweets; he was not unkind nor was he unwise, perhaps, a bit unlucky, however, in business.

Grandpa was a tinner by trade, and he established a sheet metal business in 1902 in a dark, dirty, narrow shop smack in the middle of a dilapidated row of buildings. The shop was only thirty feet wide, with tongue and grove wood floors, dingy plaster walls, and very high ceilings. The place had no office, only a plate glass window with an old roll topped desk completely empty except for a scratch pad, pencil, and telephone. With the industrious name of *J. P. Werner Sheet Metal Works*, Grandpa and his partner Cully—who somehow later became unpartnered— would manage to get jobs to install gutters or cover a roof with tin. After settling on a price, they would fabricate the material, and traipse off side-by-side with horse and wagon to install the metal work. Grandpa and his "tinners," as sheet metal workers were called in those days, would find work wherever they could. Most times the job would require only one day, but if the distance was as far as Raleigh or Frayser, it would mean spending the night in someone's barn.

We never knew what happened between Grandpa and Cully to dissolve the partnership, but as a child I saw Cully once or twice, almost blind, relegated to the simplest duty of answering the phone, which he would scream into almost as if to reach the person by voice alone. He had one bad habit, which infuriated Grandpa. Cully would routinely charge customers thirty cents for a piece of metal no matter what the size even if it was just a scrap. Ironically, the charge was exactly the price of half a pint of Lem Motlow, the cheapest whiskey available. We didn't know exactly what happened to Cully; he, like so many of the old tinners, just faded away. Grandpa also died when we were young, but not without a fight, clawing my mother's arms as he lay in the bed gasping for breath.

Our grandmother, however, lived well into her nineties. She was a dour straight-faced woman unlikely to smile. My best memory of her was on a day when my brother, Louis, and I were visiting our uncle's house on a lake, and he asked if we would like a wee snort of Jack Daniels. Grandmother insisted on a drop which proved to be three full inches in a glass jelly jar. After downing the whiskey in one gulp, she then decided she wanted to go fishing. Refusing a life jacket she remarked, "What the hell good would that do at my age?" Grandmother died peacefully at the age of ninety-four.

2

GRANDPA ALLEN: FITTING A SQUARE PEG INTO A ROUND HOLE

The Allens didn't have two nickels to rub together. Granddad Allen was Scottish but lacked their frugal ways and never earned a decent living. Grandmother was English and was only known to us by faded pictures for she had died at an early time in our young lives. The Allen women were of hearty stock and, except for one aunt, lived well into ripe old age. There was one uncle who died young in a swimming accident, an incident that pained my mother even many years later.

Granddad was the only one of the four grandparents that my brother, Louie, and my sister, Lee, and I ever really got to know. It wasn't that he was odd, but he was the poster image of a round peg that could never fit into a square hole. He was, however, one of the kindest, most gentle and intelligent men one could ever meet, and yet he led a largely wasted life. He had been a newspaper editor for a time working at offices in Paducah, Kentucky; Nashville, Tennessee; and later in Huntsville, Alabama. But as children, we knew him only as a broken old man drifting from one family member's house to another.

Most of the time Granddad lived in our home simply because we had more room than the others. This caused a great deal of resentment not only for my siblings and me, but also for Dad. The worst of it for us kids was that Louie and I were forced to sleep in the dining room, and it also forced three generations to contend for one bathroom. For Father the aggravation was of a different sort. About every four months or so Granddad would go on a little toot with his cronies. When that happened and Granddad returned home drunk tensions would flare. Dad would come home from a hard day's work having had a few snorts himself to find Granddad drunk at his dinner table. Evening meals were a sight to behold. There would be yelling and arguing about Granddad's lack of monetary contribution to the household— washing dishes and cleaning a bit was all he managed to do—and other gripes from Dad about things I can't recall. Louie and I would giggle the whole time quite likely from sheer nerves rather than any real understanding or amusement about things. But my poor sister, Lee, would be shamed to death silently praying for the tirades to stop.

There were good times with Granddad too. He was always the type of person who made you remember the good over the bad. This ability, and the memories, created a fondness in my heart for him for a lifetime.

The Depression years were tough, and we had to make do as we could. For instance, all up and down Spring Street the crow of chickens that were raised for eggs and meat could be heard. And I can recall the hilarious sight of Granddad in a clean white dress shirt wringing a chicken's neck and bird shit flying all over him and everything around him. In addition to the ubiquitous chickens in every yard, for some reason we had a goat. I doubt we used the goat for dairy products. More like the goat used us for a good meal dining on our clothes hanging from the line. So there was the usual sight of Granddad or another one of us chasing the goat around trying to retrieve an article of clothing from the frenzied goat's mouth.

Eventually, Granddad was able to get Social Security and lead a decent life. He moved into a rooming house near Southwestern College. Every so often he would implore the two old ladies who owned the house to have Amelia and I over for Sunday dinner, where he was obviously proud of us. It was, at times, embarrassing. Granddad tried writing, inventing, and investing and succeeded at none of them, but he never stopped thinking. He died a peaceful death at ninety five after his usual five mile walk.

Despite our circumstances, our good times are a testament to the solid foundation of our beginning. Our grandparents and Dad and Mom all gave us something we could not see: it was hope and strength to persevere. Besides that, as kids we saw ourselves as the same as any other. Everyone was in a similar situation and many, many were far worse off with no opportunities or prospects for improvement.

3

EAT MORE LIVER AND ONIONS, IT'S GOOD FOR THE BLOOD

Our neighborhood was between Hein Park, with its twisting streets, huge trees, and expansive yards, and Binghampton, a neighborhood with dilapidated houses in small yards with little or no grass. Hein Park was a community of wealthy, established families of Memphis' well to do, while Binghampton was populated by the down and out. Spring Street was in between.

Spring Street had a mixture of blue- and white- collar families of all faiths filling the houses and yards with herds of noisy children. The one streetlight on our block of Spring Street was directly in front of our house, which tended to draw kids like moths to a flame. Our house was situated right in the center of the block making us the focal point for kids playing in the street. Both day and night, neighborhood kids could be seen hanging right out front, unless, of course, the light was out due to our excellent marksmanship. Why kids would try to put out the only illumination on the street is anyone's guess, but we threw rocks at it every night, and the street light was out as much as it was lit thanks to us. But that never stopped the kids who gathered in front of our house.

Our house was modest, with one bedroom for my mom and dad, a second for my sister Lee, and my brother Louie and I fit into the small third bedroom when Granddad was not visiting. Granddad's periodic visits shoved Louie and me into the dining room since Granddad slept in our room when he was there. Our house, like the neighborhood, was noisy and hectic and in constant turmoil. There were arguments over who got the biggest piece of pie—when we were fortunate enough to have any pie to argue about—and who slept where, but it simply boiled down to money or the lack thereof. But even at the time, I was aware of something that separated us from other families, and that something went beyond money. We were too young then to realize what that special quality was, or even to realize the fact that we had little money.

The one thing that we had was our health, until Louie contracted Polio at the age of six. I had no idea what Polio was, only that it was very serious and very contagious. Ralph, one of the neighborhood kids from down the block, caught the horrible disease at the same time. Using juvenile logic, all the lads on the block remembered that Louie had taken a drink of water from the same glass as Ralph, therefore transmitting the disease. I blamed Ralph for the longest time, until one day, years later, when he explained the truth. He had contracted Polio in Gary, Indiana while visiting relatives, and when the authorities discovered his condition the police were called. Ralph and his family were given a motorcycle escort to the state line of Kentucky, where they were given another escort to the Tennessee state line, everyone trying to rid themselves of the young man carrying the disease. Ralph never recovered having a withered leg and used a brace for the rest of his life. Louie was put into the Isolation Hospital on Jefferson Avenue, and for some length of time no one, including our family, was permitted to visit. Our uncle Joe was a policeman, and one of my favorite people, and would use his uniform to gain admittance to Louie's floor, where he would gather him up in his arms and bring him to the second story balcony. The entire family stood and waved while Louie stood with a lost, bewildered look on his face. After months of isolation Louie was released completely cured, but surely affected in some manner. Who could say? Maybe Mom insisting on the entire family kneeling to pray every night worked another miracle.

The only one in the family who started out on the short end of the stick was my sister, Lee, but that didn't last long. The direction of Lee's life was solely a result of her own intense determination. My father was not goading her to become a tinner, mother was not hounding her for grandchildren, nor was anyone encouraging her to do a damned thing. Yet she was and still is tough as nails. Lee was small for her age but would back down to no one. She held her own in our house and on the street, which was filled mainly with boys who loved picking on the few girls on our block. Lee knew what she wanted. She was the first to work her way through college. And when she decided that she would be an artist, she went to the original Academy of Art in Memphis, which was located in Victorian Village, an area of Memphis well known today for its old homes such as Fontaine House and Magevney Place. It made little difference that she had no car. She simply insisted and, if necessary, raised enough hell that I take and pick her up. And I did. It didn't matter to her that I was busy with boxing with Christian Brothers and going steady with Amelia who later became and has been my wife for more than fifty years. Lee was determined to get things done. So when she finally bought her own car, an inexpensive old Ford coupe, I spent the next harrowing month teaching her to drive. If there had been a women's rights movement at the time, you can bet Lee would have been right out front carrying the banner, which may seem a contradiction to her artistic mind but reflects her true independence. Ultimately, Lee became a well known painter, and her paintings were shown in many galleries and today grace many homes.

All the young lads hung out together. We would all spend every waking moment outside, walking to Raleigh, swimming in the gravel pit near some factory where we would return home smelling of chlorine for days. We would go to the forests of Overton Park and build huts and smoke grapevines and have mud ball fights. Usually, someone would get hurt from jumping off the garage roof thinking he was Superman or being hit hard by a mud ball that had a rock in it. All of the kids in the 30's and 40's got their sex education from word of mouth or a from an older kid who had gotten a "feel" in a dark movie theater. And once in a great while from Clyde, who would swipe his mother's romance books from her dresser drawer, with lines describing a lass with raven hair, lying on a satin sheet with her breasts bursting from her low cut bodice, and a handsome prince about to devour her. But the first real live action was witnessed by a bunch of us at a neighbor's house. Charley, being older, knew all about sex, or so he said. He exclaimed that he could show us just how it was done. He sort of strutted to Mr. Norell's house halfway down the block dragging a number of boys, and a few girls, and the crowd growing quickly as they found out what was in store. There, in the backyard, stood a hutch with two rabbits. There was an audible sigh of disappointment. But Charley hollered, "Just shut up and watch." After things quieted down, Charley explained that one was male and the other a doe, and we soon saw why our smart ass cousin had been bragging. As the throng watched, the male rabbit jumped on top of the doe and started pumping for all he was worth, then fell off and lay down as if he were dead and the doe hardly moved. After a short while, the male would get up and eat his food as if nothing had happened, but after a short rest, he would lift his nose and sniff, then jump on the doe and start all over again. We all thought that the whole thing was pretty exaggerated if "doing it" was going to a knock a guy out. We figured Charley was full of crap, but no one had nerve enough to ask their parents.

Like all kids, we liked to play with matches. Over time, we had burned various yards and fields, then come home smelling like ashes. But only once did it do any real harm. Someone, no one would admit later who, lit a bundle of papers being stacked in our garage to be used for the war effort. The building burst into flames. The five or six of us ran around like crazy gathering up the hose trying to water the fire down, too scared to holler for Mom. Then to our horror, Dad turned into the driveway. We just knew our goose was cooked as Dad slammed the car door and ran toward us, but to our surprise, he was yelling, "Turn off the God damned water!" We did so as quietly and meekly as possible. It wasn't until later that night when the fire had demolished the garage did I overheard Dad tell Mom that the damn garage had been a junk pile, but a well insured junk pile.

The street was our kingdom. It was the place we played ball; it was our meeting place for sitting on the curb staring at the clouds, dreaming of things to come. Recently, I drove down Spring Street and wondered to myself, "How could we have played ball on this narrow street? How could there be some many ragged vehicles blocking our old curbs? And how could our once well cared for homes look so seedy and small?" Time changes everything, but still I wondered, as I drove away in my smooth running comfortable car, where all those kids are today. Certainly not on this neglected, narrow street of decaying porches. But today is the new millennium, and the depression days I remember so well are long past.

After a hard day's work, Dad would sit on the front porch in his undershirt, having another beer and talking about the Cardinal's chances for a pennant with the other dads on the street. We were afraid of Dad as kids, and it was not until many years later that I realized that he was just as afraid as we were, but for different reasons. He was just plain scared, scared about money, scared about work and scared about the responsibility of a family. He was a man with a family to feed and clothe and a mortgage payment due every month—all of that from a sheet metal shop with little work and damned little chances of getting anymore.

As I grew older and became a sheet metal worker myself, Dad and I were at constant loggerheads. It was a tough business to survive in, and the stress was tremendous. Once, after I'd become a grown man, one of Dad's tantrums was so intense I broke down right in the middle of our little office. When he saw me falling apart, he wearily dropped down in a chair, tears in his own eyes and with such a look of misery on his face I can still see today.

The term "Depression" meant nothing to us as kids. We knew there was little money, and we were only embarrassed and confused when Mom would holler, "Go see if they have any free soup bones," while at the corner store. We never wondered what to do with ourselves, instead we wondered how soon it would be dark enough to be forced indoors. In some ways the lack of money brought us closer together.

Our mother was the glue that held our family together. She stood five feet tall in her high heeled shoes, which she kept next to her bed. She put on her shoes as she got dressed, never taking them off until bedtime at night. Mom was the first up. She immediately combed her hair and put on make-up and lipstick. She loved to cook but was not very good at it. For breakfast, there was something that would stick to our ribs, such as oatmeal with milk, but for the most part she loved to fry. There were fried pork chops on a good day and fried salt meat on a bad one. If at all possible there was liver and onions, because as she said, "It's good for the blood." On very special occasions there were fried pies. I can still taste them, lard and all.

Mother had a joy for life more than anyone I have ever known, and she molded us to be more than we should have been or expected to be. She was the Pied Piper, gathering children as she went to walk the five miles to Aunt Amanda's where we would go to the field next door to chop sugar cane to eat, and swim in the bayou behind the house. She would take us to Overton Park to play something called box hockey, and we would usually get into a fight. Mom loved to wear hats, always set at a jaunty angle. What a sight it must have been to see this little ninety pound lady, with her hat set at a bias and high heeled shoes, with a bunch of kids of all sizes straggling behind her.

At night , she would sit on the porch with one of us as we poured out our woes: the loss of a girlfriend or boyfriend, or the lack of one, wanting to do something we couldn't afford, or just the frustration of growing up. She gave us her time; she gathered us together, she kept us close, she shepherded us through all seasons and changes in our young lives.

4

THE SCHOOL THAT SAT ON TOP OF THE CHURCH

We almost always walked to school. The bus was just two blocks away, but we shunned it in favor of walking the two miles or so, unless the weather was forbidding. It might have been better for us to ride than walk, since we walked through the rough streets of Binghampton each day to get to our school. Blessed Sacrament was and is still located right in the middle of Binghampton. Those neighborhood guys were tough and hated Catholics. We walked on one side of the street, and they walked on the other calling out to us "Pot-lickers," which we never learned the meaning of. We traveled in a pack, usually with an older and bigger cousin who didn't take crap from anyone, so we had very few scraps. Some of us like Louie and me were fairly small for our age but could call name with the best of them. With cousin Charley along , we'd swear—mostly using words we didn't know the meaning of—and throw mud balls as much as we liked. But as Charley grew older and was no longer in school with us, we found out just how fast we could run.

Blessed Sacrament School held classes on the second floor right above the church. Each morning we attended mass and then marched upstairs for lessons. We were taught mostly by sour-faced nuns who seemed to enjoy teaching us a lesson with a yardstick across our palms or bottoms. Although the nuns were strict, they were wonderful teachers, and I remember what a joy it was the first time I saw a picture of a mouse and realized I could spell the word. From that day forward, school was more than just merely marking time waiting for recess. I began to pay attention, especially to one young nun with a face like an angel. She reminded me of Ingrid Bergman in the movie *The Bells of Saint Mary's*. She had a disposition just as angelic, and singled me out for the much-envied chore of erasing the blackboard. My infatuation lasted until seventh grade when I went to my first party where spin-the-bottle was played. On that night, I fell in love at least six times.

Even in early grade school, there were perks that exceeded the opportunity to erase the blackboard. If you were fortunate, you would be selected as an altar boy and then you really had it made. The first time I donned the long black robe that fell to the floor and that white shirt that looked like a lady's blouse, I considered becoming a bishop or at the very least a parish priest. Being an altar boy meant serving mass in front of the whole school, always with a beautiful look of holiness on one's face then genuflecting so very slowly. Stares from covetous boys signaled their awareness that you would be saying mass years from now.

I loved serving as an altar boy. My only problem was that I was so damned small. It was always my job to light the candles before mass, but I could never reach them all. With the long wick fully extended, I went to the altar, head bent in "holiness mode," and lit the lower candles. Then reaching as far as I could, I strained on tip-toes until my legs shook, but still unable to reach the highest candle. Then my mate Bernie, a brute of a guy, would charge up, grab the wick out of my hands, and light the candle that I could not reach. I was completely demoralized. He absolutely ruined my first day as altar boy.

Bernie and I went on for several years serving as altar boys sometimes making big tips at Gypsy weddings and funerals. For some reason, they loved to use the facilities at Blessed Sacrament. Even as I served on those occasions, I had aspirations of becoming a priest though they were somewhat dulled by episodes of spin the bottle, I thought I might pursue it until we committed what was, at the time, a big mortal sin. One Saturday while in the sacristy putting away our vestments, Bernie pulled out a small vessel of wine that was about half full and passing it to me said, "Hey JoJo, let's finish this off." Not wanting to appear chicken, I drank half and Bernie finished the rest thus ending any, if even less than serious, light-hearted consideration of entering the priesthood.

Our adventures continued as Bernie and I made our way through school, even though they no longer included thoughts of becoming a priest. As we got older we began to notice those around us more and, as kids do, we began to notice more and more of the little differences among us, despite our very similar circumstances. Most of the families in our school were as poor as church mice. It was the late thirties and the very depth of the Depression in the South. Children came to class with sack lunches, some with damn little in them. Some could afford a Coke, but most were from big families and did without. I once caught my buddy Eddie gathering all the mostly empty bottles of Coke and pouring them into his own for just a sip more. Most days his sack had only a few leftover biscuits in it. But none of the kids complained; that's just how it was. There was an unwritten rule at our school: no other kids clothing or hunger was ever discussed. The nuns would put up with no nonsense about another child's condition. The dignity of each child was paramount. Once Bernie made fun of another kid's dress and by the time one of the nuns was finished beating his hands with a ruler, he had to be taken to the convent to have his hands soaked to reduce the swelling and ease the soreness.

By the eighth grade, our minds were filled with mixed emotions. There were still parties with spin-the-bottle, but girls talked less of becoming nuns, and their kisses were more intense. Boys became more serious with the knowledge that, for most, their formal education was soon coming to an end. The war was on and fathers and brothers were being killed. We all felt a clear break in the simple ways of life and the way things should be done. We were edgy. We got into fistfights. Friendships were not as close. Adult life and its worries loomed large ahead on our horizon.

I still had my paper route, but Dad was intent, as he had always been, on my learning the sheet metal trade and coming to work with him, whether I continued my education at Christian Brothers or not. Lee was in high school and starting at the Art Academy. Poor Louie was dragging behind me and hanging by hind tit. It was an awful period for me, half teenager and half child. Soon, like everything in life, it was all about to change.

5

THE PAPER BOY AND THE FIVE DOLLAR MIRACLE

For a dime you could go to the movies if you were under twelve, and if you were small like me and lied about your age, you might get by until you were fourteen. Add another dime for popcorn and a soda and you had a whole afternoon of entertainment. The problem was that we didn't have the twenty cents. As Dad would say, "Money is as scarce as hen's teeth." Most of us fought for any sort of job from selling subscriptions to Liberty or Look magazine to collecting old paper and bottles for recycling. But the job with the most prestige was to be a paperboy.

In the fifth grade I started out as a paperboy's helper. The route was in the Binghampton area, which meant walking a couple of miles to get to the route and a few more to throw the papers. After two weeks, I not only threw most of the papers but also did the collecting. I ended up doing everything for the inaptly named Dewey. He was tall and skinny and looked like a real doofus. He also had a lisp, which in that neighborhood meant that if I didn't collect we weren't going to get paid. And a lot of times we didn't. Part of the route we worked included the Collins Street Eleven, which took up one block and was a row of eleven identical houses. These houses were the hardest to collect from and I would try for weeks to get their remittance for the paper they received. No luck. I would go by week after week sometimes as many as four weeks in a row to collect. There was always some lame excuse as to why they couldn't pay. Then on the next attempt they would have gone, flown the coop. Finally, I gave up and told Dewey that I was quitting and he would have to find another helper.

It was surprisingly easy to get a route of my own, since I was now an experienced veteran. It helped that I knew how to fold the paper so that it would fly like a Frisbee. And I knew how to handle deadbeats by cutting them off. However, it only took a few days to prove that I had bitten off more than I could chew.

The new route was a morning paper, which meant getting up at about four in the morning and walking a mile to the substation to pick up my bundle, then walking back in the same direction to reach Hein Park where my route began. Hein Park was an exclusive neighborhood with huge homes and enormous yards that stretched the route out even further in front of me. I didn't care though, because I had graduated to a route where I could make a lot more money. The people in these homes had money, and all I had to do was collect it.

Our substation was in a diner run by an old Greek fellow. In the morning we would all meet at the diner and drink wonderful warming hot chocolate while we waited for the paper to be dropped off. After finishing the route I still had time for a short nap before going to school. I would rush home and stretch across my bed just in time for mother to run in and hurry me off to school.

Each weekday brought different responsibilities for me. On Sunday, the paper was so thick it required two newspaper bags strapped like bandoliers against my body, one on either side. Now that I had my own route, I had progressed enough to have my own helper. In those days it was customary if you had a brother that they help with the route. And Louie did. He struggled along, but together, bags dragging the ground, we would make our way down Broad Street to deliver the Sunday edition. Friday was collection day and we would spend our evening going from house to house gathering payments for our deliveries. Then on Saturday mornings we would ride the street car downtown to pay for our papers and then splurge a little of our earnings on a movie. Every dime was precious and we were careful how we spent it.

Collecting was never as bad in Binghampton as it was one rainy, gusty night along my Hein Park route. I collected as usual and went home. I sat down at the kitchen table with Mom as I always did to count my collections and suddenly discovered that something was terribly wrong. I had the sinking feeling that I was missing some money. And just as I thought, we discovered that I was missing five dollars. Five whole dollars, a five-dollar bill not a nickel or a dime, was missing from my collections. I was panic stricken and burst into tears. But Mother was unflappable and ignored my tears. She decided that there was no way that a fiver would not be found if we did enough praying. So we prayed to Saint Anthony, and went out into the rain to look for it. The wind was blowing and the rain was coming down hard, but Mom and I trudged back down my route in the downpour, flashlight in hand, praying like mad and searching for the money. I still hardly believe that we found it. There, lying in the middle of the street, was a soaking wet five-dollar bill. I couldn't believe how lucky I was to have found it. I had no idea how I would have replaced it.

I continued to throw my route for several more years from that point through the tenth grade. Then for the first and only time in my life I was fired from a job. It was a problem with collections that ended my grand career as a paperboy. One Friday night during my collections, a man came to the door of one of the more expensive homes in Hein Park and told me, in no uncertain terms, that he had already paid his bill. Like all paperboys, I kept a collection book in the event that the customer didn't want a punch card for recording weekly payments. I cherished that book, for it was my business record. But no amount of cajoling or whining could make the man even take a glance at my book to see that he had, in fact, not paid. Too scared to lose the money, I told the man that unless he paid I would stop his paper. Later that evening a call came from the district manager to tell me that the man demanded an apology, which was something I was not about to do. The manager was really a nice man, but the poor guy had no choice but to fire me. The only bright spot in the whole situation was that my father, who usually stayed out of such things, vigorously defended me. He had ignored my paper route up to this point thinking it beneath me, even knowing that I would soon be a tinsmith. But he wanted to beat the hell out of the manager for firing me, and it took Mom and me to keep Dad from calling and at the very least cursing the guy out.

6

THE SHOP AND THE TINNERS

Mr. Oliver, a printer, lived across the street from us. Every time he saw me he would holler at his son Johnny, "Why don't you be like JoJo and learn a trade?" But Johnny was like most of kids on the block. Being only fourteen left them with few opportunities other than throwing papers, or being a soda jerk. The year was 1944 and I was ready to start high school determined to go to Christian Brothers with its wonderful reputation, but it was unlikely that the paper route would be enough for the $125.00 tuition. That's when I approached Dad after he had drunk a couple of beers and asked him to add the remaining tuition fee. His only comment was, "Go ahead boy, as long as you pay your own way." From that day on, until well into my marriage, I became a sheet metal worker.

Every work day morning I would wake to the sound of my dad throwing up. When he emerged from the bathroom, looking a little white round the gills, his stomach had settled enough to drink a little coffee and eat some toast. Then he'd holler at me to hurry while I was still eating my oatmeal, something Mother insisted on because it would stick to my ribs. By seven o'clock we were backing out of our driveway in an old 1938 Plymouth. We drove the three blocks to pick up my uncle Louis, who was blind, standing with one foot on the curb, and one foot in the street and his wife Ruth, standing easy, holding his arm. Ruth was one of the special people in this world. She was a nurse by vocation, and had a serene way about her that could turn Louis's tirades into whispers simply by her soothing manner. She was a small town girl, took her nursing seriously, and was rarely seen in anything but her starched uniform and white cap. She knew nothing in life except how to care for others. When our daughter was born, we never considered another namesake but that dear lady. Dad would honk impatiently from a block away, even though my aunt and uncle were clearly visible. No one knew the reason for his blindness, only that sometime in his thirties his sight gradually vanished. With Louis's sight loss also went the ability to estimate, bid, and negotiate jobs. Dad had been the outside man, the guy who the men looked to for their job assignments, and to get the job done on time, and still make money. Now Dad had additional responsibilities, and it showed in his spastic driving and loud voice.

The drive to the shop had a sameness to it every day. Louis would slam the door to the car as he got in, ignoring my sweet aunt. With his deeply yellowed fingers, long and tapered much like a pianist, he'd light the first of the sixty or so cigarettes that he would smoke that day. As soon as the Plymouth pulled away from the curb, a storm would burst. The Werners were renowned as a family of yellers, and Dad and Louis certainly made their ancestors proud. With Louis screaming instructions about the day's projects and Dad yelling his disagreement, I would cringe in the back seat hoping like hell that none of my buddies were up early enough to see me. It took the whole summer for me to realize this weirdly construed method was their way of approaching a plan for the day.

As our car turned the corner and came loping down Poplar, bent axle and all, making it look much like an old hound dog with its back end trying to catch the front, one had the feeling of entering an era from a Charles Dickens novel.

The shop was fairly new, but built of cheap concrete block with the mortar still bulging from the joints and nothing for an office but a small square notched into one corner of the building and a smattering of cheap furniture. Of course, there was no air conditioning and for heat there was a small gas chill chaser in one corner. The three block area was known as the skid row of Memphis, always reeking of grime and smoke, and seemed dark even on the brightest day.

The row of buildings across from the shop were built in the early 1900's, showing every day of their age. The corner apartment was two storied, occupied for the most part by very aggressive prostitutes, who at fourteen scared hell out of me. The first floor was famous for being the hideout of Machine Gun Kelly, a notorious bank robber and somewhat of a local hero. Adjacent was a shoe repair shop run by a fellow by the name of Crow. A Russian immigrant, he was the only true communist in the area. He was a man of immaculate nature, even during working hours, and could be seen on weekends in Court Square in a black suit with a bowler hat preaching the truths of Lenin as he saw them. This obviously didn't sit well with the street people who would walk by his shop yelling curses, but very little came of it as they were usually drunk and Crow was a strapping fellow. Crow had two downfalls in his otherwise gentle demeanor. One was that he drank, not just now and then, but every day. He drank a quart of Jim Beam, the type of whiskey that caused him to loose his manners by late afternoon, when he would come to the door of his shop and shout denunciations of the United States. The other was his wife who was completely mad. She drank as well, but was less selective than Crow. She swallowed anything at hand, and by afternoon was to be seen wandering down the middle of Poplar in a filthy dress, the hem not reaching her knees, with large carbuncles on her ugly legs. She'd scream at the top of her lungs that Crow would never bed her that night unless he came up with a quarter.

Directly next door to the shoe shop was a sheet metal company and a small butcher's store. The sheet metal company was owned by a Jew with the most apt name Abe Chlem. Being Jewish in those years was even worse than being Catholic, and being a Jew in the construction business was unheard of. Construction people were Smith, Jones, or even O'Malley, but never Chlem. Didn't he know, Dad would say, that Jews had clothing stores or at least a scrap business? But Abe survived, maybe not getting rich, and owning two liquor stores certainly helped. Dad and Louis claimed he used the shop to get away from a nagging wife which probably had some merit because he chased women with abandon. Often, he was seen flying down the street in the biggest Cadillac that money could buy. Abe became a legend on Poplar when he died at a fairly young age. The rumor was repeated by the street people and shop owners, but behind the butcher's back. The rumor was that Abe had succumbed while dallying with the butcher's wife.

The crew that waited at the front of the shop were a pretty sorry looking bunch of men. These were the guys that were too old or too unfit for the Armed Forces. There were two that we called shop men, Gurley and Hank, guys that could become magicians with a pair of snips and a hand brake. They were the men who turned out the special fittings for the field men. Gurley looked like the Pillsbury boy. His head as round as a bowling ball, a protruding stomach as hard as a brick, and he was always ready with a smile. Hank was rail thin, wore an engineer's cap at a angle and had a disfigured hand, done in by an elm tree going forty miles an hour while drunk. Hank always wore Blue Goose work clothes with the shirt sleeves rolled up tight to show off his biceps and a pack of Chesterfield's stuck in the rolled up cuff. Word was that he was a mean drunk, especially to his good looking wife.

The outside crew were men who worked on the various projects, usually four to six regulars. When Dad needed more help, he picked up guys from the Union Hall.

Roy the grinder showed up most days, but never on Monday. Roy wasn't a very good mechanic, but he tried hard doing some of the rough jobs, working on a roof at ninety degrees with hot pitch swirling in his eyes.

Grinder was one of the regulars. He had been with the shop since I was a kid. On the mornings when he did show up, he stood on the corner of Jackson and Breedlove always neat and clean. Roy was a good looking man, with prematurely gray hair, but, as Dad seemed to say about all the men, "JoJo, sooner or later they just get done in by whiskey and women." One morning Grinder didn't show at the corner, and Dad, who had slowed down to look, sped up assuming that it was just another day like Monday. Later that same day Grinder came in the overhead door at a half trot, pallid, and shaky. He told the horrified crew that he had gone to the corner bar the night before, and ended up with one of the local girls, bedded her, then somehow reached his home and went to bed. By chance he awoke with an awful urge to pee and gazed with horror at Mary, his overweight Irish wife, made more undesirable by the many warts on her chin and her drooping breasts halfway out of her nightgown, straddling his stomach with bread knife in one hand and penis in the other. After much pleading, with promises that it would never happen again, Mary let Grinder go. The entire assembled crew shuddered as one, giving sage advice, saying to Roy, "Get your ass home and pack, then get the hell out of there. No way would I live with a woman mean enough to cut off a man's tally wacker." Of course, Roy was like all of Dad's crew, he kept drinking, and he kept womanizing until one hot day he was backing across a roof, walked backward, held the front of a skylight with Cal on the other and dropped through the hole he was going to cover and broke his ankles so badly that he never worked another day.

Charley was there every day, always early and always dressed in clean bib overalls. He was my favorite man to work with because he got to do the jobs that others thought dangerous. For the most part covering steeples or domes with copper, often hundreds of feet in the air. Charley looked old, though in truth he was probably no more than fifty. But he could skin up a scaffold and sit at the top waiting for me to shimmy up and sit to catch my breath. I loved working with Charley, with his quick, quirky motions. He never stopped for a break like most of the guys, knowing only one pace, which left his helper exhausted at the end of the day. He told me once that he started working at the age of six picking cotton with his mother picking along side of him, row by row, with his three siblings waiting under a tree. He only told me once, after having a few nips, that the son-of-a-bitch who was his father had deserted them, and he was the man of the house. He never did learn to read or write, but somehow that made me feel closer to a man who kept his distance yet always enjoyed my explaining some of the things I learned in school.

And there was Joe Phelps, a sweet but sad guy who was only twenty and an orphan. He had one shriveled arm making him worthless as a sheet metal worker, but Dad hired him anyway because of the way that he hung out around the shop, and never asked even though it was obvious that he needed a job. It was heartbreaking years later after we had moved to hear that Joe had gotten married and that his wife had run off with another man. That night, he came in hugged his young son then went into the bathroom and put a shotgun in his mouth.

Frank's nickname was " Bonny." He was at work most days but barely able to make a go of it. He had a short stint in the Army and was discharged for what was finally diagnosed as cancer of the stomach. Frank was dumb as a post, an absolutely wonderful baseball player, a horrible tinner, and a mean drunk. He had been with the company from the time that he had quit school in the ninth grade where he had been for three years. The word from Dad was that he had an arm as good as Ty Cobb but was likely to throw a man out at first base while a man on third stole home. He was strong as an ox and when drunk would fight anyone including the boss. As a little kid of ten or so, I rode in the back of the truck while Frank rode shotgun as we ran down to Walls, Mississippi in order to finish a little tile roof. Somehow, Frank got some whiskey and by the time we got him home he was out of his head trying to pull poor Dad out of the truck. Dad and Frank's wife, Angie, finally got him to go inside, but not before he knocked poor Angie down, no mean feat since she weighted a good two hundred pounds. Frank was even worse with a hammer and chisel than me. While cutting mortar joints, he would miss about every third blow, but unlike me, he would ignore his bruised hand, never missing a beat. At the end of each day, he would wrap the mitt in cold cloth and do the same thing all over again the next day. Even as young as I was, I saw no discernable reason for keeping someone as useless as an old mule and sometime just as contrary, but that wasn't Dad's way. He was just as loyal to his men as he was softhearted.

Pear's given name was Otto Herman. He looked as German as his name, was round as a butterball, stood five nine and weighted about two hundred and fifty pounds. He wore a size 48 belt, hence the nickname, and had been married at least one time, producing a surprisingly pretty daughter. He was neither neat in appearance nor in workmanship. Pear probably couldn't have kept a job anywhere else, but his toothless grin and his willingness to tackle any job made him a favorite with Dad and the crew. He ate every chance he got. He told me once, "When I was a kid JoJo, we never had enough to eat, and now I just can't seem to ever get full. I just want to eat all the time." Often I would work with Pear, since we both hung out with the gutter crew, doing the more simple type of work. We would leave for the job early in the morning with me sitting in the bed of the pickup with Pear, his belly in his lap, almost losing my breakfast as I watched him stuff his jaws with souse and crackers, the juice running down his chin. Pear acted as the ground man soldering the gutter into long pieces and installing down pipe tubes, while the rest of the crew climbed the extension ladders and hung the gutter to the eaves of the roof. He was a surreal sight sitting cross legged on the ground in a yoga position, his wisp of hair hanging down, his belly hanging out, looking all the world like a Buddha. His soldering looked awful, but was always watertight. Since Pear was older and had been in the first World War and had a fear of heights, he was not asked to climb the thirty foot extension ladder to hang gutter. On only one occasion did he have a problem. Dad had landed a huge job at the Naval Base installing gutters on a number of barrack buildings, a job that would last all summer and required four men. On this day, there were only three of us, since it was a Monday and Grinder had not shown up. Cal had a twisted ankle, which left only Pear and me to hang the gutter. With the two ladders in place and the gutter ready to hang, I grabbed my end, and thirty feet away Pear grabbed the other. He stood there looking up at that wobbly old wooden ladder, hitched up his pants and started to the top. But halfway up disaster struck when Pear's pants fell to his ankles. First, there was shock at the sight, but after a moment, I burst out laughing and my laughter got Cal started, which left Pear completely helpless. After we finally righted ourselves, Pear pushed and pulled until he got his pants back in position. In the end, Pear accepted the laughs like he did everything, just giving us that toothless grin.

There was Chester, a kleptomaniac and someone I really didn't like or trust. He came from a family of no accounts. He had a sister who was an absolute doll, but the other men warned me away, especially if I had any money. Chester looked like a movie star, with a good looking wife. Duke, his father, always had a babe half his age on his arm. The whole bunch stayed in trouble with the law. Even after I was married, Chester called me one night to bail him out of jail for being drunk and shoplifting. Over the years they all drifted away, we heard to Chicago.

Cal was always there even when not needed. There was an understanding that if a man showed up, he was put to work even when there was none. Cal was a real asset for doing manual labor, since everything was done by hand. There was no power equipment for shearing or folding metal. If we needed such things as flashing or gutters, we used hand snips to cut the sheets into strips and then took them to a huge hand brake where we stood, hour upon hour, pulling down the clamp to hold the metal in place, then pushing a large ball used for counterweight to fold the metal into shape. After standing at a table for eight hours cutting the metal with a pair of snips, like a woman cutting cloth, my hands would turn into fists on their own. I dreaded working with Cal at the brake for an eight hour day. He was a stoop-shouldered hulk of a man, with a gold front tooth, which he loved to exhibit. After a full day, when I could hardly stand upright, Cal would casually walk to the front of the shop at quitting time waiting for the rest of the crew. The ritual ahead must have been on his mind for some time, since his yanking the counterweight quickened as the day wore on.

Every afternoon was an affair that bordered on celebration. Someone, usually one of the men coming from a job, had stopped at Solomito's Liquor, and by half past quitting time the crew had circled one of the work benches. The cap had been removed from the bottle of bourbon and discarded. The men with great dignity would pass the bottle from hand to hand, squinting through the brown liquid making damn sure that they hadn't taken to big a swallow but to be damned sure that they had taken their share.

7

THE ESCAPE FROM ROME
AND LIFE UNDER A HOUSE

The twenties had been good to the Werners. Grandpa was German in every sense of the word when it came to good workmanship. And as Dad and Uncle Louis took the reins, pride became a part of each project. Buildings of import were all throughout Memphis: the Peabody Hotel, Southwestern College, the Exchange Building and others. Among these buildings and large homes was found much of the handiwork of *J. P. Werner Sheet Metal Works*. Glazed tile, grey slate, copper gutters, fancy ornamental heads on drainpipes were all over Memphis. As I grew and became a teenager, my future was already decided by my dad. On weekends, Dad and I would drive the various project sites, and he would point at buildings and homes on every corner, "We done that," he would say. No matter how much pride and attention to detail went into every job, it was not enough to save the business through such tough times.

The Depression ruined what had been a flourishing business. Construction in Memphis went from boom to bust in a matter of months. As a result, Uncle Louis ran the office and the few small jobs that remained, which left Dad to search elsewhere for work and any sort of pay. Through his various contacts, Dad was able to find a large project in Rome, Georgia.

The year was 1936 and we loaded up and left in a vintage Model T, driving along a road built mostly for horse and wagon. It took two days to get there, and we stayed in rooming houses along the way. The cheaper the better. The entire family in one room. The bathroom down the hall.

The whole experience was beyond description for us kids. We had never been out of the city before and would not be again for many years. Just on the edge of town, we settled into an old house situated on a mountainside. I remember walking out onto our back porch and looking up at the boulders directly above the house and wondering if they would fall on the house. Aside from our surroundings, little changed. Dad still came in dog-tired at night, and Mom—hat, heels and lipstick in place— still led us kids everywhere. She took us all over the city. A favorite spot was a cemetery high atop a mountain where we would picnic and play hide-and-seek among the tombstones.

With things still very much the same, it was not long before the work ran out, and we were on our way out of Rome. Dad's work seemed to end abruptly, so it was time to traipse back to Memphis. And we did so: in the middle of the night. As we kids curled up in the back seat with Mom looking frightened, Dad packed us up and drove off from the deserted town. I can still hear him saying what he repeated to Mom all that night, "It's alright, Nora, once we get across the state line the police can't do anything to us." Years later we found out the reason for our midnight escape. It seems that the landlord had insisted on a full month's rent for the few days extra we had stayed, and apparently Dad had in response threatened the man with bodily harm. At that point, our adventure had ended, and we returned to Memphis. But the whole event made for a great story, and it was a joy to tell my tale of midnight escape with police in hot pursuit to the gang on Spring Street.

Nevertheless, we might be saved from our dubious fate yet. As the Depression waned in the late thirties, construction picked up especially in building churches and other houses of worship. It was a time of screaming preachers insisting that people give more to build bigger and better churches. They were needed to house all the hordes of worshippers who were praying to stem the living hell which they had survived. And it was this very biblical building boom that put *Werner* back on track.

By luck if not by design, the Werner company became the company for the job. Whether Protestant, Catholic, Jew or Greek, these buildings needed sheet metal and roofs. The Baptists had dipping pools with steps lined with copper. The temple and synagogues had domes covered with tile. And the Protestants had steeples. For years to come steeples grew taller and taller, and *J. P. Werner Sheet Metal* grew busier and busier.

As an apprentice sheet metal worker—boss's son or not—I didn't start on those lofty buildings rising a hundred feet into the air. Instead, I began my first summer before high school under a house. In the early forties, older houses were in need of having coal furnaces replaced with natural gas. I, along with Chester the kleptomaniac and one-eyed Cocky Henson, would crawl under houses everyday and pull out old pipe and replace it with a new furnace plenum, ductwork and grills.

Each morning that summer began the same: a quick stop at the liquor store for my coworkers and then under the houses to get covered with dust. Twice during the summer, I had to stop Chester from stealing at a customer's home. At one house, he wanted to steal fuses, and another time, he tried to steal the family photo album.

I swore I would report him to the homeowner if he tried it again. Cocky wasn't dishonest, but he had the horrible habit of removing his glass eye and wiping off with a filthy handkerchief and placing it back in its socket. As the day wore on, each man began to get on my nerves and work more slowly. Chester would get sleepy and Cocky would start telling the most outrageous stories I'm sure were all lies. Somehow we managed to get the work done, eventually. And there was no point in complaining or ratting on them, for they would only be replaced with the same type of worker with the same or worse habits. And as Dad said, "The choosin' was down to the nubs."

8

DAD- THE ICE WATER-
AND THE WET CAT

Ninth grade started with a fight. Many of the boys at Christian Brothers were from well-to-do families, and within a week a couple of sophomores with that pedigree decided to pick on a kid too small to be a freshman—me. I loved to fight like the other boys from my neighborhood, so being asked to meet at the railroad tracks behind the school suited me just fine. It was early in the school year, which made for a small audience but that mattered little. And with a wallop, all the frustration of working under a house for three months came out of me in furious blows. After a quick scrap, I had whipped the one who had been pushed into the fight by his friend, and the friend decided he wanted nothing to do with me. Later that same year, however, the guy that I'd had the scrap with was giving me a ride home every afternoon. He had simply been a young man trying to

49

prove how tough he was. I'd wait with him until his alcoholic mother would pull up in her big old luxury car, that was a bit worn looking, to drive us both home. Many afternoons she would stop at the Cotton Club on Parkway and have several drinks before heading home. Ted and I would drink our Cokes a few seats away from her and talk quietly about the future.

After such a dramatic beginning, it was surprising how quickly school turned dull and routine. At home things were always more lively. My sister was always begging Mom to make Louie and me leave her and the other grown ups alone when she had the girls from Immaculate Conception School over to spend the night. Louie was at Blessed Sacrament School and still young enough to get away with pranks. He especially enjoyed the occasional prank that he could pull on Dad. Louie had one standing order, which was to fix Dad a glass of ice water each evening and bring it in to him while he listened to his beloved Cardinal games on the radio. On one particularly hot night, Louie went out the back door and crept to the back window where he knelt and began to howl like a cat in heat. The racket lasted until a huge glass of water went flying through the screen drenching my brother as Dad calmly laid back and resumed listening to his baseball game.

I was too old for such silly pranks and didn't have much time for them anyway. The paper route still kept me busy, though not for much longer. I worked every chance I got as a tinner. Any extra time I had was spent at the corner drug store lounging in a booth discussing girls with my buddies and lying to each other about the sex books we had read. It was a time in life when nothing seemed to go right. You didn't get the things you thought you were entitled to: new clothes, spending money, or a car. You're embarrassed about your parents and their clothes and their car. Your parents didn't understand you, and they won't give you what you want or deserve: typical teen behavior no matter what generation.

Although hormones and puberty create a natural restlessness, I had become especially belligerent to Dad, blaming him because I was not able to do some of the things the other boys could do. I had to work when others were sleeping until all hours on Saturday. There were more fights at the railroad tracks behind school, and I was running around with the wrong crowd. And I had started smoking—something my mother detested.

9

WHISKEY HALL AND DOWN–AND–OUTER'S GOTTA EAT TOO

There was a clear distinction between sheet metal companies. Within an area of six blocks, there were five shops. Two were much larger than the others and located closer to downtown Memphis as if to disassociate themselves from the old tin shops like Werner, which seemed to fit into the dingy surroundings of skid row. We were the old; they were the new. And with the new came new opportunities for new work.

All the many large office buildings going up were air-conditioned, which required duct work, but Dad hated duct work and so did the men who worked for him. Truth be known Dad and Uncle Louis didn't know a damned thing about duct work. It was completely alien to them, and there was not one piece of equipment in the shop to make the pipe and fittings. All of the power tools to turn out duct work were damned expensive-just too much money they both decided. There was plenty of other metal work to keep us busy: steeples to cover with copper panels, shingle flashing, gutters, tile and slate roofing—plenty of work to go around for all the shops. So we took jobs we wanted and the others we left. Dad was looking to me more and more to make decisions. Dad said more than once, "I'm wearing thin JoJo if you want to fool with it that'll be up to you." Dad really did look like he was wearing thin sometimes: all those years of working on a roof, of trying to make payroll, of putting up with wayward men. The stress was taking its toll on him, and he depended on me.

I was becoming a good mechanic: Gurley and Hank continued to pound at me to pay attention and learn, knowing that I was their future. They were two of the best mechanics in Memphis. These were the sort of men that commanded an extra quarter an hour over the union scale-something Dad couldn't afford. Yet, both men were like all of his workmen and remained loyal. Dad made Werner's a place where a man could earn a decent living and be treated with dignity even as a tinner, which was damn hard work.

Sheet metal work was unique in the construction business. Everything started with a flat sheet of metal. An elbow or fitting was laid out in gores much the same way a tailor lays out a pattern for a suit or a seamstress for a dress. It is a time consuming intricate operation that requires a precise hand. After being laid out, the gores were cut by hand with a pair of snips, rolled on a device to seam it, bent in a hand brake, and finally, soldered together piece by piece. One small mistake and an entire sheet of metal would be ruined. Neither of these guys were kids, yet they could make a reducing elbow for a tug boat while it waited in the Wolf River harbor and have it finished in time to be for a drink at four-thirty. They worked together like a well-oiled machine. The only competition between the two was for the prime workbench directly in front of the plate glass window where they could watch the parade of winos, high-steppers, and occasional thug that passed by. Together they worked productively for Werner's for years until later when Hank lost his mind to venereal disease, and Gurley died of liver failure from all the whiskey. But when I knew these men, they were helpful to me almost to a fault.

When I wasn't lucky enough to be learning layout work, my days were spent cutting strips of metal with a pair of hand snips. With no power tools, tinners like Cal, whose hands never seemed to wear out, would cut hundreds of feet of flashing to be installed on a school or church. Usually, my old snips would leave a jagged edge, and the metal I cut could be traced by a trail of blood left on the edge.

Dad usually left the shop early each morning, and with his exit, there would be a huge sigh of relief. Uncle Louis, who had been arguing with Dad a few minutes earlier, would turn on his old box radio tuning the dial until he got some good country music. Then he would stand in the front door and smoke. Using wooden kitchen matches long enough to prevent burning his fingers, he would strike them on the blackened doorjamb. During the four or so hours that Louis stood sunbathing, holding his blind eyes toward the sky-a trace of a smile on his face-a panhandler would usually inch up and ask for a handout. If Louis was convinced that the bum was serious, which was based on whether or not they reeked of booze, he would summon me from my bench and hand me fifty cents with stern instructions, "JoJo, go next door and buy this guy some food and wait for the change." When you are a kid and you have a bum dogging your heels begging for the change you duck your head and do your best to ignore him, but I would walk them to the café to get a meal. When I entered Nick's Café next door, I was greeted with laughter from the layabouts that seemed to make Nick's their home. One thug by the name of Birmingham, who was a big and burly guy and enjoyed telling dirty jokes in a loud voice, would make fun of the boy of fourteen charged with the duty of feeding a bum. I hated it and dreaded making the trip into Nick's until Cal happened to hear him one day and slapped him with an open hand full in the face. I always thought to prove what a coward Birmingham was. Although, Cal may have just had a belly full of the drunken display of a fool who would drink each day until he was unable to get up from his chair. Whatever the reason, from that day forward, there was quiet if not respect when I brought my bum in to eat.

Inside the café, Ms. Mary greeted me as if it was the first time I had stepped into her café knowing I wouldn't want to chat with the bum in tow. No one knew anything about her or her family. She had a son and a husband, neither of whom was ever seen. It seemed the café was always open, and she was always behind the counter ready to serve a hot meal. I wondered sometimes if Nick was her husband or her son and why she didn't name the place Ms. Mary's Café. Mary was a tiny woman hardly reaching five feet tall with peroxide yellow hair. She wore bright lipstick and a white uniform that made me think she had aspirations of becoming a nurse. She even had a sterile quality about her like a nurse as she moved about behind the counter serving her patrons. Ms. Mary fixed a hot plate lunch, ignoring the odor, and served the man with a patient smile and then quietly slipped me the change. She was used to it, for my bums were not the only down-and-outs who crossed the threshold of her door.

It was a most peculiar neighborhood. Despite the horrors of poverty and despair brought on by the depression in all my years working at the shop, I never witnessed a fight of any type. The drunks were men and women who had suffered through the depression and would never recover. They had given up. It showed in their stoop-shouldered walk and care-worn faces. When they asked for a handout, unless they were already drunk, it was with downcast eyes. Of course, the handout was for a drink; something to transport them from the life they lived and expected to live until they died. And death came much quicker than one might expect in most cases.

Once on an early morning when Dad had driven off to make his rounds, Louis and I happened to be the only two in the shop-that in itself a rare occasion-an ex-tinner who long before had given up work to pursue the bottle came into the shop by the overhead side door. His nickname was Whiskey Hill, and he was so in need of a drink that he almost danced across the floor shaking as he begged my Uncle for money to get a bottle. His request was denied by Uncle Louis in a voice so loud and harsh, it made me wonder if he was recalling his hangover days. Whiskey's shaking soon turned into tremors so bad I had to help him to a bench. He sat for a short time and then asked to use the toilet. Work was waiting, so I went back to my bench and Louis to his country music. But within minutes, Whiskey came flailing out of the little bathroom, his entire body going in different directions as if he were coming apart. With me holding on as the man seemed to be having an epileptic fit and Louis threatening to call the police, Hank, another shop man, came in from a job and took over. He laid Whiskey back on a workbench in another room. Shortly, Hank came out with an empty pint bottle of rubbing alcohol. I didn't see it, but I guessed that Whiskey drank it. Although, I put in my two cents worth and said he looked pretty near dead to me, Hank and Gurley decided that Whiskey was all right. But he had hardly moved all day, just twitching slightly every once in a while. At four-thirty, the men took him outside the gate, sat him on a concrete block in the mid-summer heat, and went home. I never saw Whiskey again, but he did quit drinking. I remember thinking to myself that if that episode didn't do it, nothing would.

The turnover of street people was extraordinary. A new bunch would drag up and down the four blocks that made up skid row. The women were usually better kept than the men, but within a few months both would have a worn-down look. On days when it was extremely hot, the poor souls lined the curb, heads down, feet in the gutter waiting for some sort of deliverance. Often Abe Chlem, from the shop across from ours, would make a call. Soon the Black Moriah would arrive and herd everyone in for a ride to the clinker, giving the street people at least a place for the night, a meal, and getting them off the filthy streets.

The only people who seemed unaffected by the dirt, grime, and general dreariness were the prostitutes. The rooming house in which they lived was off limits for their use in entertaining men, and in fact it was occupied by families including children. The women were clean, happy, pretty individuals who seemed to take pride in their profession . Many of the young girls destined for this life would disappear at a certain age and reappear a few years later looking exactly like their mothers. In an odd way, however, there was a kind of code that governed the street.

There was a certain element of pride, that was revealed by skid row's inhabitants, which often showed itself in small ways. You wouldn't expect a community of prostitutes, drunks and hardened men to display a code of ethics, but I remember clearly the summer that proved just that.

A new shop had recently opened run by a sleazy looking man and his dumpy, mustached wife. They rented a tiny store, and filled it with nothing but cold drinks, candy bars, and potato chips. The place was located a few doors from Werner's. Inside it was so dark one could hardly see to make a selection. Almost at once the kids were hanging around and looking for drugs. As bad as Poplar was, there had never been drugs of any kind on the street. That was something seen only on Beale Street or South Main. To make matters worse, there were hints of young sex being peddled within the tiny, dark shop. At times, one might be waited on by the woman in a bright, flowery dress with a face painted heavily enough to hide the dirt. As she rung you up, she would have her arm around a young lad of twelve or so sitting on her lap, a glazed expression on his face. On other days, one might enter and find the same young lad or an identical type sitting on the flabby, fat man's lap who was her husband. The boys seemed to be on display along with the snacks and drinks. This brought the whole neighborhood to an uproar. The men at Dad's shop, the street people, the drunks, even the whores were up in arms as if to say, "Enough, we don't want that kind of crap going on in our neighborhood." Soon, after months of threats and bottle throwing and broken windows, the two took the hint, closed up and moved away.

Those were unforgettable days: all the characters from the neighborhood and all the strange events. Hank and Gurley and the shop men regaling me with their wild stories of conquests and exploits-exaggerated for my benefit. I was growing up right in the middle of it all. I remember the feel of the breeze drifting through the shop, even the country music, which I usually disliked but gave Louis so much pleasure.

10

THE WASTED YEARS

The end of the Second World War meant little to our family. We were the lucky ones. None of us had been killed or maimed like many of our friends and neighbors. Things had become better for Werner Sheet Metal. A resurgence in the construction business made it easier for Dad to find men and material.

A war that had cost millions of lives had been waged and our family hardly knew it occurred. We were so tightly wound up in our own world and cares that little outside of our immediate circumstances punctured our consciousness. Only once did I have a personal experience related to the war. A year before the end of the war while working on a large home installing a tile roof, I was told to be as quiet as possible because the lady of the house had just received a telegram informing her of the death of her son. In that one instance,

I looked at that sad woman, not much older than my mother, with lines etched into her face and felt her sorrow. But I also felt guilt. My only excuse for being insensitive was lack of communication in the forties. There was no television, and radio could not make the tragedies and turmoil of battle come to life for me. Newspapers listed the dead and injured, which failed to convey the searing pain of loss felt by suffering families. Our only outlet was the news at the Saturday matinee, and even it had a sameness to it that began to wash over us without really touching or engaging us in the realities of war.

Even without feeling the impact of the war in a deeply personal sense, life seemed muted, dulled by the difficulties and hardships of the day. School had lost its appeal for me. The Brothers, who we had listened to so earnestly for years were losing their solid and unshakeable image. Many of the Brothers were scattering to other parts of the country, leaving the order. It made one wonder if being a Brother had been a excuse for avoiding the Armed Forces. Even those men who were committed to teaching and less interested in discipline displayed furrowed brows of anxiety and less patience with students than usual. Two of my favorite Brothers left the order at the same time. Brother Daniel, who looked young enough to pass for a student, decided to move away and get married. And the other, Brother Marcus, simply decided to leave the order for reasons unknown. Before leaving, he'd begun walking like an old man. His face looked sad and no longer approachable and friendly as he had been in the past. With school becoming less interesting and the disappointment of my favorites leaving, I began to focus on more important things—girls.

We all began to take dating seriously. I was going out a lot, and just beginning to do some serious necking. I wore myself out staying out too late, spending all my money and finding it to be a hell of a lot more work than I thought. The time was past when we rode a bus for two hours to take a girl to a movie, hoping for a chaste kiss after the third date. But no one in our crowd could match Clyde. He was not attractive in the least. He was a big fellow of six three, and had an awkward build with all that height on a small boned frame except for his big feet. He wasn't much of an athlete, which could instantly make a guy popular with the girls. Yet somehow he got by, had money without ever having a job and was an item with the girls. While the rest of us would spend our money courting girls and trying like hell to get past first base, Clyde would show up at school with bruised lips and still half asleep. It was not unusual for him to have two dates a night, though he never bragged about it. He would simply be more tired than usual the next day. I don't know how he did it, what he said or what he promised those girls, but it worked. Monday mornings he would show up at school with lips that looked like he had been eating strawberries from all the smooching and necking he had been doing. Most of us spent that school year in dazed confusion, almost getting in trouble but not quite, almost getting a girl in trouble but not quite and trying to decide what to do with our lives after graduation. I knew that Dad expected me to be in the sheet metal business after high school, but I looked at my buddies and knew that I wanted to be like them and go to college. Our generation just coming out of school was going to have to learn how to compete. There would be a lot of competition with the end of the war. We were apprehensive.

There was, as there always is, constant change. Things were busting out all around us, and it felt like madness let loose. Guys were coming home from the war hitting the ground on the run, anxious to make up for the time they had lost while we sat on the sidelines. Sixteen is a tough age for anyone, but for us it was especially tough. Guys returning from the war were going after our jobs and our girls, and they were tougher and more savvy than us. There were a lot of fights over girls or simply as a result of the frustration that we felt. We'd get into it on the gravel parking lots of the Cotton Bowl and Duke's Drive-In, and when that happened we usually lost. I tried to steer clear of it, and I thought I could do a better job if I had my own car and wasn't riding with other guys more inclined to get into a mess.

After my unending pleas and Mom's intervention, Dad gave in and decided to teach me to drive. The next two weeks were terrifying. Dad would take me out every day after a beer or two and do his best to be patient while I made a mess of shifting the old floorboard mounted gearshift. The car sounded like a cement mixer as I shifted from gear to gear. I'd stick my arm out improperly for a turn and generally play havoc with the rules of the road. Dad, bless his soul, was trying too hard to teach me the simple elements. The harder he tried the more nervous I got. Finally, he would lose it and blow his cool and yell. But because that was Dad's way I actually felt more comfortable with him barking orders like a drill sergeant and within a few weeks, I got my license. I could borrow the family car in most cases after agreeing to take or deliver something or someone, somewhere. After doing so, my date and I would end up with another couple necking at an outdoor diner or drive-in movie. It wasn't as hard to get girls, since I had transportation. But it was still just as hard to get past first base with or without my own car. But man, did we try.

Once in a while we would go to one of the drive-ins where the so-called "bad girls" hung out. They were the girls from what we considered the wrong side of the tracks, or the wrong side of the river. If our hormones had not been almost out of control, we would probably have avoided such places since there was a good chance of getting into a fight. At some point during that school year most of us ended up with a girl who had a reputation, a girl with a name like Dee Dee or Tammy. For months at school we'd hint around that we had gotten a long way past first base. But most had not.

September was always a good month. It was time to start school again, time to have some freedom with guys my age away from the old men I had been working with, time for some of us to get away from our jobs and have fun. It was the month of the Mid-south fair which meant a week of spending every minute away from school, traipsing up and down the midway, traveling in a pack and scrounging for the abundance of small town girls. We felt and acted like big town guys-wearing our purple and gold sweaters-condescending to entertain a bunch of young kids who had ridden to town in an old yellow school bus with names like Pontotoc High stenciled on the side. Little did we know that those cute, buxom farm girls, dressed in their best clothes and traveling in packs, would back us down with their frankness. They knew what they were looking for, showing no anxiety, and serious as a heart attack.

As the year went on we began to experiment. We learned to drink at the Green Beetle on South Main. It was our routine to get a bum to go to Frank's Liquors and get us a pint of sloe gin. It was the accepted drink of the young and a vile tasting sweet drink which had the effect one expected: to get us drunk. Then we would get sick and brag about it for a week. The Beetle was a true joint with all the dirt and noise, and supposedly off limits. There the sophisticated girls who were slumming, and girls who the slummers were trying to imitate, could be found. Punks like Crazy Cal hung out at the Beetle. Crazy Cal was a notorious nut case who, if he couldn't find anyone to fight would put his fist through a wall. He was the sort of thug who became meaner with drink ready to hit anyone no matter his size. Years later, he married a beautiful girl who he used as a punching bag until she eventually ran away with another man. But not everyone in our crew was as crazy as Cal.

There was one fellow in our bunch who was always on the fringe and never took part in our silliness. He only seemed amused by it. Kenny was a well built, slender sort of guy, usually wearing a coat and tie. His appearance was altered by a terribly pock marked face, which seemed to bother others more than it did him. Kenny was older than us. He had been in the Armed Forces and attended classes at odd intervals and was never seen in a joint without a drink in his hand. Kenny was polite to a fault, ready to help anytime. Once when Crazy Cal, who outweighed me by fifty pounds, decided that since I boxed he would see if he could knock me across the room. Kenny stepped in and fought Cal trading blow for blow. When the fight was broken up by the police Kenny was still standing and went back quietly to his drink. In the years to come Cal would go to prison, while Kenny would be seen coming out of a joint sober, dressed in coat and tie, and always alone. I never felt as if I knew Kenny. His half smile seemed to hide a loneliness none of us could touch. I felt as if I was missing something very important, that I had slipped and missed an opportunity not getting to know Kenny. But that was one of only a few things that I would take for granted over the years.

It was the year we began talking about integration. Most of my buddies knew nothing about black people. There was not one black person that attended the Brothers, and none of us had even known one socially. This was not the fault of the Christian Brothers. It was simply never thought of either by blacks or whites. If a young black lad had applied they would have been welcome. The Brothers were truly color blind. It was a period of truce. Everyone wanted to get along. The war was over, and for a few years people just wanted to relax and enjoy their freedom. Being around black roofers since my early teens had made me as unbiased as a human could be. It was degrading to me for an old roofer having to address a young kid as mister. For that short period it was not as issue for us, but it was an issue that one of the generations behind us would have to come to grips with.

It was a time in life when we were lost. We went steady because it was expected of us, and we had long discussions about our future with our pals or our girlfriend. We all wanted to go away to college and get out from under our parents. In truth, it was a completely wasted year: a year of hopes and dreams, and misery and talk and no action.

11

BIG YELLOW AND THE MEN WHO WERE NEVER PRAISED

Werner was spreading its wings. Bidding on jobs in outlying areas of Memphis, like Ripley and Brownsville, meant different sources of income. But little else changed. The projects were much the same as the ones done in town: slate and tile roofs, gutter and flashing installation, covering steeples in copper. Projects were estimated in the same way. Estimating was a mixture of eyeballing the plans and then measuring the amount of material with a scale rule, then arguing back and forth between Dad and his loyal customers. But nothing was really changing, nothing important. The shop was still not equipped with any sort of power that would increase efficiency or productivity. The office was tiny and uncomfortable, and the whole operation seemed to lack progress in meaningful ways. On the roll topped desk were folders, but no contracts. Dad would do it all in a handshake at most and more often than not the work started when the project was ready. A man's word was his bond. Dad knew it, the contractor knew it, and they lived by it whether the job was in Memphis or elsewhere.

Dad probably slept very little on those nights when we were working out of town. I would leave home at five or six most mornings and not return until late evening. My dad had a habit of waking me up at four or so, and I in turn would show up at one of the tinner's houses to wake them. Grinder, Do-Right, Cal or Charley would stumble into the living room where I waited half-asleep. Then the man whose sleep I interrupted would take me in with a look that could kill. With their hands shaking badly from a hangover, they would disappear to get dressed. Together, we would make the rounds picking up the rest of the men, and eventually head to a job site fifty miles away. The larger sheet metal shops in Memphis had a simple rule that men show up at the site at eight o'clock, but the Werner crew had no transportation.

The ride to the site was an adventure in itself. The old Thirty Eight Dodge pick-up had gone to its death years ago. It was replaced by a succession of used trucks, each lasting a year or more, until a high pressure salesman got a hold of Dad. The result was a bright yellow Ford one ton with side panels. The truck rode as if it had no springs. It was impossible to load it down so that it would not bounce so terribly. The ride was never smooth. Everything bounced: the men, the material and me. I was the innocent driver, but was blamed for each pothole and rut when heads hit the roof as I chauffeured my hung-over passengers to our destination. If headaches didn't ensue from the ride, they would surely be festering by noon in the scorching heat.

It was a summer from hell, one of the hottest in Memphis history. The Werner crew spent it on flat roofs installing flashing and gutters, chiseling mortar joints with a sledgehammer, and mounting gravel guards. The roofers, like us, only spoke when necessary conserving energy and knowing from rote exactly what came next. Each knew his job, while also anticipating what the others' needs were. We covered ourselves in Vaseline to keep the pitch from burning our skin, but often we would go home with burns that would scar like huge birthmarks. Tempers were short. A man might walk by another barely touching him as he passed, a man he drank with every night, and a near fight would erupt. The heat, pitch, fumes, and fatigue took the men near insanity. But a friend would always step in and things would be calmed for the moment.

The mainstay of the group was the ground crew. Without them there would be no roof. The kettle man, usually an older man, was the key. He knew when the kettle needed turning up a notch to keep the pitch boiling, and when to add a block of sold pitch. With the kettle man was a young helper just learning. The helper would pull buckets of gravel up by block and tackle, and would fetch the solid pitch to be added to the kettle when it was called for. Unfortunately and all too often, he'd burn himself when the boiling pitch splashed. This was no easy job even though these two men were not on the roof; they could never stop and lean on a broom to catch a cool breeze. The ground crew had to keep going all the time, making sure that the tar and gravel got to the top of the building for the proper completion of the roof. But the final responsibility rested with the foreman.

The roofing foreman, the only white man on the roofing crew, would sit on the firewall smoking a cigarette with his wide brimmed hat down tight and sunglasses pressed close to his head. Occasionally, he would look up checking to see that the pitch was being applied in just the right amount because he knew the final product was his responsibility. The foreman looked just as miserable as the men working around him. And if there was trouble he was the first to step in with a helping hand. At noon, he would climb down from the roof and sit on the ground with our crew. He would talk about the farming community he had escaped, while I thought to myself that he had merely gone from purgatory to hell.

Words of praise were never given to those roofing men with little or no education. They were the men who kept the pitch bucket from swinging near me. It was a simple courtesy with no need of acknowledgment then, but in retrospect I'd like to thank them. They took no notice of the color of my skin. They worked hard and would not last long. Many would die in their forties half-blind with half a lung, with a family to support. At quitting time they would take from their overalls a half pint of whiskey or a pint of cheap wine and take a long pull on the bottle and smile. They were the men who did what was necessary; supporting their families and never complaining, knowing that there was a job to be done. Not one "thank you," and little rest.

When the day was done, the ride home was rough, potholes and all. Sun was beaming directly into my eyes as I drove west, home to Memphis. Sometimes I would nod off, only to get an elbow in the ribs, "Wake up damn it, and drive!"

12

THE STEEPLE JACKS

Dad never specifically asked me if I wanted to work on a particular job. My first thought when he called me into the office was, "What the hell have I done now?" Instead, very un-dad like, he said, "Freddy's been hurt, do you feel up to climbing a steeple?" My first inclination was to smile. But I could see that Dad was very serious. For a moment the fear showed in his eyes; I could see that he considered the job a dangerous one. So I just kept a straight face and said, "Give me a minute to get my tools together."

Because Freddy was hit in the head by a falling two by six I became a steeplejack. The job was a church near Southwestern College where Charley was waiting nervous-as-a-whore-in-church, pacing up and down. He wanted to go back up top now that he knew Freddy wasn't badly injured. Truth be known, Freddy should never have been on the steeple in the first place. He was strong as a bull but deaf as a post, and, being deaf since birth, his speech was impossible to understand. Freddy had a gash on his forehead, but he had gotten to the ground on his own. Except for a few stitches, there were no lasting ill effects. It did, however, give Dad an excuse to let Freddy go, since he had always known that a deaf man should never have been working on such a dangerous job. Dad found Freddy a job with a plumber, and for years we would see him at the street dances on Court Square jitterbugging like a professional with that goofy grin he always had on his face.

Riding out to the job with Dad, his hands clasping and unclasping the steering wheel, I realized that he was much more frightened than I was. I realized for the first time in my life what a softy he really was. No other shop would think of hiring a deaf kid who couldn't be understood, or a young man with a withered arm, or guys who would be thrown off the job for being drunk or not showing up at all. I was finally seeing Dad as a man who had too much shoved on him all his life, and yet could feel compassion for others.

When we arrived on the job site I put on my tool pouch slung low on my hip like the gunslingers of old, except my pouch carried hammer, folding rule, and tongs. I swaggered over to Charley. Without a word the fifty-year-old climbed directly to the top, grabbed the crossbars of the scaffolding, pulled himself up, then waited patiently for me to reach the top plank. Many times that day Charley asked if Freddy was all right, and I could hear in his voice that he somehow blamed himself.

There was work to be done but for a minute I wanted to sit on the scaffold board and look out over the city. I was seeing Memphis as I had never seen it before. What a clean, fresh feeling. What a wonderful view with all the trees in full blossom, a sea of green, red, and bright yellow. It was one of those feelings that Memphis has in the fall—a nip in the air, a perfect day, a day that makes one feel almost majestic. What a sense of freedom I felt. Charley must have seen my exuberance since he didn't say a word. He just smiled a little, as if he could remember the first time he climbed a tower, and after a minute said, "JoJo, let's go to work. We've got a steeple to cover."

Spires had become a fad, a symbol, becoming taller and taller as if they were trying to reach the heavens. All over the South churches were going up; in the smaller towns, in outlying areas like Atoka, or Covington, or Tunica. The steeple might be a squat, four sided figure, built of paint grip metal, but in Memphis where the real competition began, the steeple had as many as eight sides covered in multiple shaped pieces of copper-etched with muriatic acid to add aging then topped with an elaborate cross.

Charley was a wizard at covering steeples, no matter the configuration or material. I became more adept as I watched and learned. Almost always it was only the two of us. Starting out early each morning, we would arrive at the job site and Charley would scale to the top while I would bundle the copper, water bucket, and lunch pails into a block and tackle. We rarely came down once we were in place. If I were half asleep when we started, it quickly disappeared when I sat on the plank high above with a feeling of peace settling over me as I gazed out on the horizon.

We became a good team. I began to see Charley for what he was, a man who had known nothing but work, could not read or write, could not drive, had a wife but no children, drank very little, and relished being on top of a steeple. It was a simple man's passion. As we finished a job he would sometimes frown as if he hated to let the job go, afraid to finish another steeple and run out of steeples before he ran out of time.

Architects were in competition with each other, just as the churches were, to use unusual designs and material. The Catholics had their Cathedral on Central; the Greeks had their church on Highland. These were very ordinary, unpretentious buildings. The Greek Church had a brick bell tower and a copper dome with a simple cross covered with the same material giving the entire structure a shrugging of the shoulders effect. Some of the other churches reflected more imagination like shingles cut from pre-finished aluminum or copper cut into diamond shapes then beaded together. Those were hell to make watertight. There was one spire that was the envy of Mississippi, which had a gold plated fist with the index finger perched atop the steeple pointing toward the heavens.

Steeples had become a tool for the church to raise more and more money, and the taller they got, the more impressive they became. Once, as we were finishing a steeple on Park Avenue, a television truck arrived along with the minister of the church. He explained to Charley that he was going to ride what we called the headache ball at the end of the crane and set the cross in place with his own two hands. After the man had wiggled the cross into place, Charley and I simply fixed the mess the minister had made, not saying a word and shaking our heads.

There were few problems that couldn't be solved with a little common sense. We were once in a small town in Mississippi installing a copper steeple on a pretty little church, almost capping out, when the builder pointed out that the cross that we were about to install was incorrect. In fact, the plans showed a ball at the base of the cross and what we had didn't look like that at all. But before the builder left the job site, Charley asked if there was a hardware store in the area. After the builder departed, Charley gave me instructions. When we left that afternoon, the pretty little church that sat back from the highway among the trees had its copper steeple pointing into the sky with a brass cross on top and a copper ball from a toilet bowl valve at its base.

One morning I was still half-asleep, dreaming of the girl I'd had a date with the night before. But I knew that I had to get to the church on Walnut Grove early that morning, and as always I followed Charley to the top of the steeple. Charley had used the ladder attached to braces, but like I did every day I simply used the cross bars which was faster but required more youth to accomplish. When I reached the top bar and pulled myself up, the weld broke free and the bar was in my hand and I was free falling. Charley hollered to me to grab something. After falling six feet, and working off of pure instinct, I grabbed a brace, hung for a minute, then climbed to the top and sat on the scaffold board with a pale-faced Charley. Everything seemed fine but within minutes I was shaking so badly the board was doing a dance. Needless to say, little was accomplished that day, and the two of us never mentioned what had occurred to anyone. After that we tended to watch each other more closely.

Charley and I continued to cover steeples. Years later they became a manufactured item. They came in sections and were much less expensive, but they all looked alike. This proved Charley somewhat of a prophet when he said he was afraid that he would outlive his beloved steeple work.

13

BOY MEETS GIRL

The day was scorching, like most days in July, when Dad called me into the office late one afternoon and told me to go to Solari's Grill to repair a stainless steel sink. Not restraining my anger, I threw the fire pot, charcoal, and soldering outfit in the truck and took off burning rubber in the old truck. I drove to the Grill and parked in the rear. I went in and, slamming the door behind me, crawled under the sink to look for the leak. I found it and re-soldered the drain. I was mad as hell because I would be late for my date with Linda. She was the pretty, chubby-legged majorette from Tech High who I had been going steady with for a year.

I was on my back below the sink checking the connection and I thought I was dreaming when a voice from above said, " What in the world are you doing down there?" What I was doing was rushing to fix the damned sink, so I could get out of there. But, what I perceived as possibly a voice from heaven, belonged to a pair of rather thin legs in white socks and penny loafers. And what I saw when I pulled myself from under the sink was a really cute girl with blue eyes that made me melt. She was the same girl that I knew to be Mr. Solari's daughter and the one that I saw in church every Sunday. It was obvious that Amelia was flirting, trying to start a conversation, and considering the way I looked I didn't know why. I stood there feeling like a fool in a pair of filthy jeans, grease up to my armpits, and the jeans ripped all the way up the seam exposing my shorts. For months, I had stared at this girl sitting with her family at 8 o'clock mass, always in the same pew, on the opposite side of the church from where the Werners sat each and every Sunday. During all those months, I had the impression that Amelia was far too young for me, so I would egg on my brother Louie to ask her for a date thinking that they might be about the same age. Now she was standing in front of me telling me she was a junior at Sacred Heart. She was only a year younger than me, and my first thought was that she was going to be my girl. The more we talked the more I was determined not to leave until we had a date. And when I blurted out, "Think you might like to go to a movie next week?" I was greeted quickly with, "Sure, what night?"

We leaned against the now repaired sink and talked about nothing. We both began to get flustered. We made lots of eye contact until I knew that I had better leave or kiss her right there in the kitchen. I got in the pick-up with Amelia smiling, leaning forward to touch the hood as if to stop the truck from moving. I slowly pulled away with sweat running down my face and butterflies in my stomach. I had just spent thirty minutes with a wisp of a girl that I would spend the rest of my life with, falling in love over and over again.

I should have felt badly about Linda that night. I picked a fight as soon as I picked her up. I should have felt remorse for the way I treated her in the weeks that followed, but Linda had become an afterthought. Amelia and I became inseparable within a month. We wanted to be with each other every minute: to touch, to kiss, to feel, we were in love. At times when she was waiting for me to arrive, her mother would admonish her saying, "What in the world is wrong with you? You're shaking like a leaf." I loved the way she looked in her bright yellow dress. When I mentioned it, Amelia wore it until it was tattered beyond repair. Sunday was our day, the one day in the week when school or work didn't interfere. I walked from Spring Street to Amelia's house on Court after church. We would have the entire afternoon to go to the Ritz on Poplar to see a movie, or the drug store on Madison for a malt. Most every week ended in a little arbor in Overton Park just sitting there holding hands with embarrassed grins on our faces, afraid that someone in passing would notice and make fun of us. Amelia was the first person that I had ever been with that I felt no need to force conversation. We simply enjoyed each other in silence. It was all childish and foolish, and it has happened to many others, but we were special. We were in our own little cocoon where no one could touch us.

Gradually we began to talk about ourselves. Shyly at first, afraid to break the shell we had built around ourselves, but soon we were sharing lots of stories. I told her about the boxing matches I was into and bragged about the steeples I scaled each day and my childhood with a street full of kids and pranks. Amelia would look at me in bewilderment and say, "I don't know what you're talking about." There were no kids on her block. There was no childhood. There were no playmates. There was only a mother who had Amelia late in life and had little time for her. The mother who fed her soft-boiled eggs and dry toast every morning then dropped her off at school on her way to the Grill. She told me that as a child she had no chums, only a school that she detested. She once said, "Mother would drop me off at school early each day, and I would lean against the dirty, yellow brick wall of the gym and close my eyes. There I would daydream until the school day started. Try as I might, I couldn't get my eyelids to open, because if I did it would mean going into that awful place to face the nuns."

14

BOY AND GIRL FALL IN LOVE

No one would ever know how Amelia had become this sassy, inquisitive young girl if they were to visit her house on Court Street. It was a self- made duplex that sat up on a small hill with a deeply slanted driveway in a quiet neighborhood. The house was considerably larger than the Werner home, but it lacked the life that our family home exuded as if the house were unoccupied.

The Solaris' home had once been a single dwelling, but by simply closing off doors and adding a wall here and there it was converted into a duplex. Mr. And Mrs. Solari lived on one side and on the other lived Amelia's brother Al and his wife Virginia. The two had eloped at the age of eighteen, finished high school, and moved in with his parents. Al was eleven years older than Amelia and handsome as a movie star. He had been a fighter pilot in the war and flown in bombing raids over Germany. Al never discussed the war and kept most of his thoughts to himself.

His wife Virginia was a no nonsense type of woman who accepted her role as mother of two, housewife, tutor and second mother to Amelia. She took her role seriously as substitute matron of the house by handling all the household chores without complaint. Al had a dull retail job with Sears but one that gave him security. They skimped wherever they could. Al even rode a puddle jumper to work every day.

Mr. Solari was full-blooded Italian. At some point, and no one was sure when, his family had emigrated from Milan. Mrs. Solari was Irish; she was a Flynn before her marriage, and her ancestors had come over from Cork. I never once called them anything except "Mr." and "Mrs." I was always uncomfortable around them. Mr. Solari owned a restaurant, and his wife spent most of her time there.

Solari's Grill was a place known all over the city where the best spaghetti was served. It was located on Madison near downtown, only a few blocks from city hall and the courthouse. The grill was extremely popular among lawyers and politicians for both its food and its laid back atmosphere. Mr. Solari was short and rotund with just a fringe of hair around his face. He was usually seen with an apron on and an unlit cigar in hand. The place opened only for lunch, but the pasta was so time consuming to prepare that he would leave home at five every morning and return no sooner than eight or so each night. No one, not even the family, knew the recipe for the wonderful sauce that made his spaghetti so popular. Some said that Booker, who had worked for Mr. Solari for years, had happened upon it while piddling around with herb and spices. Others said that Mr. Solari had brought the recipe from the old country. Whatever the truth was, the grill was a huge success. People would start coming at eleven sharp. Most all of them ordered spaghetti, some with meatballs or ravioli.

On Sunday afternoon, if the Chicks baseball team were in town, Amelia and I would be treated to the use of the Solaris' big old Packard car. We would drop off Mr. Solari at Russwood Park on Madison, a baseball field with dilapidated wooden stands, where he would sit alone in the same seat chewing tobacco, and holding an unlit cigar. The two of us would use those few hours to drive around, me steering with one hand while I had the other around my girl, and feeling to all the world like some big shot.

Mr. Solari had good reason to enjoy baseball. Some years before, both he and my dad had played together every Sunday morning after church. They played in something called the "Bushaw League" at Hodges Field on Jefferson Avenue, across from Veterans Hospital. The "Bushaw League" was the oldest organized baseball league in the United States, becoming well known nationally with the rosters filled with ex big league players. As a young man Dad had been a hell of an athlete and played center field, and Solari was a catcher. Dad was fast as greased lightning and Solari, when he had his gear on, looked like the poster for a big league catcher. As a child I would ride with Dad each Sunday morning and sit on the bench, filling the role of batboy. Most of the men had a chew of tobacco in their jaw. I chewed gum, but I could spit with the best of them. It was the happiest I ever saw a bunch of men: cussing the umpires, running the bases, letting themselves be free for a while, as if to say, screw the depression. It was one of the few times I saw Mr. Solari smile. He would raise his mask after a good play at home plate and grin with pure glee.

By the time I reached high school both men had retired, taking the role of spectators. Mr. Solari had grown tired from too many long hours at the grill. And Dad, on a day that I was bat boy, was hit in the nose by a fly ball, which caused two black eyes. I remember him saying later, "I saw two balls JoJo, and I reached for the wrong one."

Mrs. Solari was an older, heavier version of Amelia. She was most certainly different, yet had some of the same mannerisms. She had a great smile, a prissy walk, and a way of throwing a hand at the ground as if to shoo away something unwanted. She also had strange habits. I learned after the first few visits to watch before I sat, since

Mrs. Solari changed the furniture around almost daily. She also loved to tinker. The Solaris had an old Magnavox radio with legs that raised it to a height of three feet. One day, when the saw was handy, and Mrs. Solari was in the mood to alter, she cut the legs off to the cross bar, a matter of two feet. Mr. Solari spotted the sinking radio as soon as he walked through the front door, and yelled "God damn it woman, what in the hell have you done now?" With anyone else, that would have been the end of the matter, but, since the saw was still handy, what Mr. Solari observed when he came home the next night was a radio with no legs at all, only the old Magnavox sitting on the floor.

We were a determined twosome. Amelia was finishing high school and had no desire to attend college. I was busy, boxing two or three times a week, working at the shop, and trying to figure out how I could afford college. And yet, every time we were together, we did nothing except talk about getting married. The little world we were in stayed intact. We ignored our friends, choosing to go places by ourselves, never bored. If I had no transportation I would walk home through the park late at night, dog tired, while Amelia sat on her porch swing watching until I was out of sight. We just simply refused to tire of each other, and never have.

15

HOW TO GET A BENT NOSE

Bevo was one of the best boxers Memphis ever produced, and it was pure chance that Dad hired him just as I was beginning to get serious about boxing. Uncle Joe, who was always trying to help someone, called Dad about hiring Bevo. My uncle said that he had been discharged from the Navy, and needed a job. Bevo was very well known and had developed enough of a reputation as a serious fighter that the crew knew he had been a golden glove champion. All of us expected a big bruiser rather than a short, heavy-set twenty-five year old man. When he came into the office, his demeanor surprised us. He had a shy but ready smile and a high pitched, almost girlish voice. His face was round, his shoulders thick. His hair was sleek, shiny and black. He kept it pulled straight back, giving him the appearance of being part Indian, which he was. Despite his unexpected demeanor, his build was more like that of a fighter, and the more we got to know him, we discovered he was not only a good fighter but also a good guy. Because of that, we became friends.

Boxing was the only sport that I was good at. I was far too light for football and disliked wrestling. Even though the Brothers were famous for both, I would make a name in boxing. I was quick with my hands and strong for my size; however, I knew nothing about style. So I saw my friendship with Bevo as a chance to work out with a semi-pro, learning how to use my hands and feet the way I had seen him work in the ring. He floated around, jabbing and dodging, hardly touching the floor. Little did I know that Bevo was in the first stages of crippling arthritis, which had forced him to be discharged from the Navy, and eventually would force him to quit any type of physical labor and give up the fights.

I had been boxing for a couple of years. I worked out at Gaston Center and Dave Wells Gym, two of the toughest places in Memphis. Both buildings were old, unkempt, and dirty, with low ceilings and lots of racket. They had no facilities except for the basic requirements for boxing; a ring, a punching bag, and a bunch of tough mugs without jobs who were ready to brawl. I had asked Clyde, my best friend for years, to act as my sparring partner until I found out he was more interested in scoring knock-outs outside the ring than helping me pursue knock-outs inside the ring. Although his six-foot-two-inch tall, two hundred-twenty frame looked muscular, he was almost feminine, lacking any physical strength or agility. However, Clyde proved to be much more effective as a trainer, holding the body bag while I pounded away for hours, taking my smokes away, stopping me before I could take the first drink, and forcing me to run laps and take Amelia home early at night. Generally, he kept me from doing all the things that he did with abandon.

While working out at Gaston one day, I found Jimmy. Jimmy loved to fight as much as I did. He was one grade behind me at the Brothers, but the same age. Jimmy was a hunk of a guy; he looked like he might have been born to fight. He had failed a grade and wasn't much of a student, but boy could Jimmy fight. We would take off every day that we could and head for a gym. There we would beat hell out of each other, or get into the ring with one of the South Side boys at Gaston or the Humes boys at Wells. They all had nicknames like Bulldog, Butch, and Killer. They were boys from tough schools unlike a school that raised boys to be gentlemen like the Brothers, which produced a boxer with a name like JoJo.

Jimmy was tough as a dime steak, didn't know the first thing about boxing, but like me made up in determination what we lacked in style. He could take a punch better than anyone I had ever seen. When he took a really hard hit, all it seemed to do was make him mad. Once at Gaston while sparing, a kid landed a knock on his head and Jimmy went wild. Before we could pull him off, he had damned near killed the guy. We both had grown up in the construction trade. We had seen ironworkers sit around a fire in the rain, get bored because they couldn't go up top and work because it was too slick, and instead pick a fight with their best friend just to have something to do. We were like those ironworkers and just loved to fight. Both of us hated to lose and never did. During those months Jimmy could beat hell the out of anyone he fought and never seem to get a scratch. In contrast, my nose inevitably got in the way of someone's fist, and eventually it sort of leaned to one side of my face. It served as evidence of my days as a fighter that would last the rest of my life.

Mr. Timkin, an ex-pro who had the face to prove it, ran the gym at Gaston and loved to work with young fighters. He couldn't have been much older than fifty but looked and moved like an old man. But when it came to taking care of his fighters, he was quick to see that we got matches any time we wanted. He worked long hours and couldn't have made much money, but he would stay at the gym keeping it open so many hours that I sometime wondered if he slept there. It was a real treat when he would round up four or five of us and pile us into his old Ford station wagon, and head for the fights in West Memphis, Clarksdale, or Jackson.

When Bevo came to work at the shop the timing couldn't have been better. I had learned all there was from Mr. Timkin, and I was sick of sparring with the same guys every day. Fighting in the small towns had gotten to be a bummer because I would usually end up fighting some kid younger that wasn't any good. A fighter, any real fighter, likes a challenge. And with no challenge, it's no fun. So I picked the right time with Bevo, working together in the shop bending a large piece of sheet metal, and I asked if he would train me for the city championship that was to be held that spring. Bevo, who had a habit of bending his face toward the floor and looking with his eyes skyward gave it some thought, and finally asked, "You sure you want to do that JoJo? It'll take a lot of work." I quickly answered, "Hell Bevo, I've been fighting for a year and got nothing to show for it but a bent nose, and, by the way, goddamn it, quit calling me JoJo." After that we were off every Saturday morning. I would meet Bevo in the loft of Humes High School where he and his best friend Sonny Boy Shelby would proceed to beat hell out of me. Sonny Boy, like Bevo, was one of the best athletes to come out of Memphis. Bevo was short and stocky and looked little like a boxer. Sonny Boy looked like he could knock over a tank and probably could. Years later, the two of them would be inducted into the City Hall of Fame.

Saturday mornings would start with each of them hitting me with jabs I never saw. Then they would make me jump rope until I felt like my legs would fall off. Next, I would hit a body bag until I couldn't raise my arms. And then they would finally turn me loose, only to wait for the next week when the two of them would start the process all over again.

While I was training with pros, Jimmy had left Gaston and gone back to the Brothers where he was working out with the rest of the guys at the school gym, getting ready for the preliminary fights. There were a bunch of lads trying to make the boxing team that year, possibly because an ex-boxer instructor from the Naval Station had taken over the program. Hopes were high that the Brothers would produce some winners, something they had never done before. The gym was packed with guys of every size and weight the day I first showed up. But it turned out that most were welterweight and lightweight—the weights Jimmy and I fought in.

The preliminary fights for qualifying for the City were held in the Shelby County Building at the Fairgrounds. Jimmy had two fights and I had three, but actually there was little competition. Most all of our matches were with a boxer who either liked to fight but didn't know how or wanted to show off for their buddies or girlfriends. They were bad enough that both of Jimmy's fights were stopped. One slim, long-legged guy I fought was pretty good, but I won easily. Another I knocked down, and the fight was stopped. Only once did I hurt someone: it was a fight with a guy I really liked, a guy who I had homeroom with at the Brothers. He left an opening and I threw a left, smashing his nose. It was something I never would have done on purpose. I was hitting by instinct.

When our team was complete, the Navy instructor, who had been a good boxer for his fleet and won the welterweight division, had us working out every afternoon. He had a real skill for teaching young men, encouraging us, and making us feel good about ourselves. I could see that for a change the Brothers had a good bunch of boxers with a solid chance for winning. The matches with other schools would start in two weeks. My first fight was with a guy from Tech, and after training with Bevo for two months I was ready. Clyde was working hard at being a second, wandering around the ring between rounds with a towel over his shoulder, something he had seen someone do in a movie. To make himself look more professional he bought a bottle of ammonia, which he kept in one pocket, giving me a whiff if I took the slightest hit. The only person not too excited about the bouts was Amelia who had never seen me fight, but had seen the results. When I came to pick her up with a black eye or plaster on my nose she would gasp, and as she saw my nose start to lean she began to cry. She never said a word, wouldn't even discuss the matches, and refused to go with my family on the night of my first fight.

Butch, the kid from Tech was not very good, and I stopped him in the first round. Unknowingly, he gave me one piece of advice after I won that stuck with me. "I thought I had a pretty good punch until I fought you," he said, "but your face never changed expression when

I hit you with everything I had." What Butch didn't know was that he had a damned good punch, so I tucked that piece of information away and from then on I kept a face like granite, no matter how hard I was hit. My next fight was with the champion from Humes, "Bulldog Wilson." He and his brother had won respective weights for the last couple of years, and I was as surprised as anyone when I stopped him in the second round. Clyde and my family went nuts. Jimmy and Bill, another Brother's boxer, both won by knockout. For the first time the Brothers had three guys in the finals.

The City Championship was a big thing in the forties. It was held in the Ellis Auditorium before a packed house. Both the Commercial Appeal and the Press Scimitar newspapers covered it. I was to fight a kid from Messick High, a good fighter with a long reach, named Bruce. Jimmy had to fight a guy with the nickname "hook nose" and Bill had drawn an unknown, sort of like the three of us. I was the first to get in the ring, since the fight card started with the lightest weight class. Thank God the emcee didn't introduce me as JoJo, but as Joe Werner from the Brothers. Bruce and I stood toe to toe for the entire fight. He was a good fighter, forcing me to jab with my left the entire fight, which was something I didn't like to do, and he hit me so hard a few times I almost went down. At the end of the fight we were both so exhausted that we each stumbled across the ring to our corners. In the end Clyde, who waved his towel at the drop of a hat, had his towel in his pocket. When I was declared the winner by unanimous decision Clyde went wild. I guess I did too, but I'm still not sure that I won the fight. Jimmy won his bout by a split decision, and Bill knocked his guy out. And for the first time the Brothers had three city champions.

That night was one for kids like us. The three of us in years to come could look back in wonder. Jimmy, son of a carpenter, Bill, son of a plumber, and JoJo, son of a tinner, all had golden gloves, and the school had a trophy. Amelia never did come to one of my bouts, and I never said anything about it to her even in jest. She had come from a different environment; one less rowdy, less rambunctious, it truly hurt her to see me hit. But she wore my golden glove on her bracelet, and showed it every chance she got.

16

DECISIONS DECISIONS DECISIONS

The excitement of the last four years was almost over. We felt confused. We were being pulled at from all sides, our class disintegrating, everyone going in different directions. The Brothers, who at one time we had looked on as something of a mockery, had stepped forward trying to help us decide where our future lay. They knew that this was a special class. There were the depression kids who had worked their way through school, the fairly affluent kids, who in some ways had it hardest of all, their future already decided, all wanting to make something of their lives. Yet there was a determination in this class, Brothers' class of 1948, something in our mixture that made us special. We were the kind of class that leaves its mark on a school long after graduation.

At the end of the year, there was the usual prom. We spent more money than we could afford to for a corsage, tux rental, and the cost of a party room at the Peabody Hotel. Once there we would sneak into the men's room to have a drink. Later we would throw it up. We were trying to act like grown ups and instead acted like fools. Girls like Amelia would sit dumbfounded by the sight after having worked days on getting their hair just so and spending money on frilly dresses looking forward to an evening of romance, only to watch their guys act like clowns. We held our girls too tightly as we danced and jitterbugged much too fast. In the end the girls would be mad, the boys would be sick and all felt miserable.

By the end of our senior year, Clyde had become a real drunk. The more he drank, the more he chased skirts, any skirts, which usually meant some guy beating the hell out of him before the night was done because he had messed with the wrong girl. Clyde had a brilliant mind; he read Browning and James Joyce, made straight A's when he felt like doing the work, but he had a hollow leg. He had a drink in his hand most of the time and would cross the street to flirt with a female, young or older, pretty or plain. He had an insatiable appetite for whiskey and women. At the time, Clyde was my best friend. We had been buddies since we were little fellas. He was the best man at my wedding, and he was usually with Amelia and me on weekends with a different girl in tow on each occasion. During rough times, it was almost like the three of us against the world.

But gradually, Clyde let himself slip more and more. He became a real bore, a slob rather than the life of the party, alienating all of his friends, including me. During the coming years Clyde was married six times, was a successful, then unsuccessful lawyer, and died of a horrible infection of the colon. While speaking to his first and my favorite of the wives, Martha said to me, "I'll bet they didn't need to embalm him, his arteries were probably filled with Jack Daniels." It was an unfortunate end for a guy who made unfortunate choices.

It was a time for decisions. All of my friends were going away to college— something that just wasn't going to happen for me. I really wanted to go to college, but Dad thought it was stupid. While working for him that summer, we had many a row. Dad would say, "JoJo, college won't help a goddamned bit in being a sheet metal worker," adding, "If you want to go to school, go to William R. Moore and learn how to read a blue print." William R. Moore was a technical school, a good one, but I wanted to make something more of my life than being a tinner. Finally, it was a discussion with Amelia that produced a plan. Amelia and I sat on her front porch one evening and talked it all through. She was far from being smart in school, she just wasn't interested, but she had a wonderful capacity for cutting to the bone with practical answers. Together we made the decision that I attend Memphis State for a year and then get married. That way, she could finish high school, and I could get a taste of higher education. I loved to read because it fueled my imagination, but if truth be known

I had no illusions of being a part of a scene from *Goodbye Mr. Chips*. In reality Memphis State was a good urban college populated by no nonsense ex-GI's who were not ready for the dull routine of class and pimply-faced teenagers from small towns who were not used to the big city or a big campus. Amelia and I had made one other decision. I had already applied with a correspondence school. I would begin courses by mail as soon as we were married. It may not have been what I wanted, but at least it would be an engineering degree of sorts. It was a decision that gave me a sense of letting my breath out after holding it too long. No more stomach aches from worry, no more hollering with Dad. Now I had a sense of security, a sense that I was making progress, a sense of direction that I had not had in prior years. Maybe others wanted more, but I had my girl and I was going to at least get a few years of higher education.

It was a near perfect summer that followed. The one thing that spoiled it was sex. Actually, it was the lack of sex. We were trying our best to act and think like adults. But truth be told, we were just kids. We said to each other that we would never go "all the way" before marriage. But on a hot summer night, sitting on a dark front porch with everyone else asleep, hormones racing, and long pent up desire, we would reach the breaking point over and over again, until, drained, we would keep our promise.

That same hot summer had brought in guys like Bevo, who didn't drink, smoke, or cuss and Curtis, and ex-navy man like Bevo, with the same positive attitude. Unlike Bevo, however, Curtis loved women, all women, which caused an itchy situation when one of the wives of a rounder came into the shop. The hot weather seemed to make the women horny, and Charley would say to me in his usual frankness, "Those girls ain't being serviced JoJo." It was probably true since their men were soused most of the time. And, it was no surprise when one of the wives openly made a play for young Curtis feinting surprise when her husband emerged from the back of the shop. Whiskey Hall's wife was a good looking woman, a real high stepper, and she knew it. With him going on a tear every few months, the obvious thing happened. Whiskey came into the shop one morning, drunk as a skunk, and confronted young Curtis. He was so out of his head that Louis called the police, which broke some sort of code that said the police just weren't called to skid row. Although the men in the shop objected, the paddy wagon carted Whiskey off. But when it became an apparent habit and happened for a second and third time with different wives, Curtis left town abruptly for California.

For Amelia and I it was the best summer of our lives. For weeks time seemed suspended, hanging in the air waiting for when our world would change. I valued Bevo's opinion, and we talked about the possibility that I would advance in the Golden Gloves and go to St. Louis for the regionals. I continued to spend some time at Dave Wells working out, but my heart wasn't in it. Then when a kid two years younger and ten pounds lighter than me asked me to work out with him and hit me so hard and fast that my teeth rattled, I decided to quit. So, I spent my days on roofs and steeples. But there were fewer of them spent up top and more doing layout work. I was becoming a pretty decent mechanic and Amelia had a job at Goldsmith's downtown at the handkerchief counter where she made fifteen to twenty dollars a week, a job she was quite proud of. They only put the prettiest girls at the counter to attract men who might be willing to invest up to three dollars for one handkerchief. The job didn't last long. Amelia and the other young lasses were given the pink slip because, as she said, the lady over them was jealous and "ugly as homemade sin." I had loved her having a job, something that gave her a little independence. We would meet after her workday and go to a movie at the Lowe's Palace or Warner Theater, two of the most elaborate buildings on Main and then eat at Britling's Cafeteria, a high-class but inexpensive place. We would walk sometimes in the evenings in the warm summer breeze and talk of our great plans for the future.

It was also that summer that I had my first real taste of bigotry. We had been taught by the nuns and brothers, and especially by Mom, to pay no mind to nationality or color. During the depths of the Depression people of all color would come to the back door of our house to ask for food and be served with a full plate, even if it meant adding a little more water to the soup. People like us weren't taught to think a lot about other races or colors, we didn't have time for it. One of my father's best friends was a Jew, and my girl was a Dago, and we thought nothing of it. There was no malice in our words or hearts, but there were others whose words and actions were full of hate. It was for that reason that I got the living hell beat out of me. On one of the nights when I left Wells after working out, I was followed by another car almost all the way to Amelia's house. I only wondered a little about it, but a week later when the same thing happened, I kept slowing down and finally pulled over somewhere in Midtown. Three guys jumped from the car and started toward me asking what I was doing fooling around with a Dago girl. I should have said nothing; I had no idea who they were, but like most fools would, I ran straight at them. The fight was short and I got much the worst of it. Then the three of them casually got in their car and left. I was pretty beat up and still mad but never told Amelia, letting her think I'd had a tough scrap in the ring, and the worst part was the punks got away with it. But that was all right. It was only a small hiccup in our lovely summer.

17

GURLEY TAKES A FLYER

My year at Memphis State was a complete waste of time. The subjects that I took could easily have been ones from my senior year at the Brothers. All of my buddies had gone to schools away from Memphis. Amelia was finishing her senior year, anxious to get her high school diploma, show her back to the nuns, and get on with life.

I found myself sitting in the library staring at the wall, lonely for my pals who were four hundred miles way at UT, or some other distant school. Most had joined fraternities, and I had been approached by two or three groups to pledge one, but I found the guys far too enthusiastic and silly. It was to most of the students some sort of status symbol, but to me it was a childish waste of time.

The two of us were starting to put money away, just a little at a time. Most of all of my classes were in the mornings, so I could work in the afternoon, and Amelia was working part time at Goldsmith's.

The boom in Memphis was about to begin, soon to eclipse the years after the Depression. The young guys had come home from the war, getting off the train with their feet running before they hit the ground, feeling as though they may not deserve the whole hog, but expecting to get a large part of it. The period of euphoria that everyone felt when the war first ended was over, now the guys who were received with a kiss and a hug wanted more. They came home and made babies. With babies on the way they felt as though they deserved a home, and a job with a decent wage.

The young bucks were starting to take over the unions, and the name Werner Sheet Metal meant nothing to them. They cared little that Dad had been one of the founders of the sheet metal union in Memphis, or that he had been an officer, and helped write the by-laws that protected their jobs. In a matter of a few years, the young turks would kick out the business agent and put in one of their own. After that their only concern would be money and a new contract every couple of years, one with a healthy raise. Loyalty was a word to be left in a book.

New trends were coming, and Dad and Louis had no answer. They were still taking jobs too cheaply, but not realizing it. Each time a job came out in the Builders Exchange I would push them to put in a bid to the various contractors. The general contractors were men like the new generation of tinners, be damned with loyalty or the assumption of a job well done. No thanks, just how cheap is your bid? No more of this crap about a man's word and his handshake being all that was necessary. Now there were long contracts sent through the mail stating "whereas", and "whereof"—words that Dad and Louis didn't understand.

On a Saturday morning when there were only the three of us present the sad comedy would begin. In that vomit colored lime green office Dad and I would pour over the plans. We would try to figure out where the flashing went, or the gutter, or other pertinent sheet metal items. We would explain to our blind man Louis, who, being the only one of the three that read plans properly, could only try in his blindness to envision the structure, while both of us talked at once. Soon the room would fill with smoke from Louis chain smoking, and the yelling would begin. Within the next couple of hours I would put figures down, multiply by hand, then add everything on a hand cranked adding machine and arrive at a bid. And somehow, between a blind man, a man with an eighth grade education, and a confused youngster, we would get the job and maybe make a little money.

There were still some of the old deadheads around, men that Dad knew well and Louis had been friends with in his carousing days. When one of those contractors had a job on open order, Werner was likely to do the work. With the more aggressive shops doing the larger projects, it at least kept the wolf away from the door.

We kept the same men, who were getting older, but no less reliable. Every so often Dad would add a young guy to replace a rounder who had fallen by the wayside. Many of the men who I had considered old when I began work as a youth, now seemed not old at all. They were, after all, only reaching middle age. Some like Hank, Bonnie, and Roy the Grinder were gone, dead, or disabled.

Either Werner Sheet Metal was lucky or Dad was perceptive. The men that he hired as apprentices and mechanics like Bevo, Young Roy, and Buck wanted to be a credit to the trade, to do work that had made the name Werner mean something. But Dad was worn to a frazzle. He didn't play ball anymore, but he still drank his quart of beer in the afternoon, and Louis drank his quart of milk each day, and they were both getting a pot belly and showing their age. But Dad still had Gurley, and Charley, and Do Right, and Pear, and Abie Chlem still had some of the old heads. A lot of the young ones settled in, maybe not becoming part of the crew that I had grown up with, but not afraid to stand around the bench in the afternoon passing the bottle from hand to hand until it was empty.

And thank God things happened as it did one beautiful morning when Louis was standing in the doorway, face toward the sun, the never ending cigarette in his hand. A nice looking man walked up with a bundle in his hand. Gurley and I were the only two in the shop, me working at a bench, and Gurley inside a large fitting that he was assembling. At the sight of the man Gurley stooped down, making his round body as small as possible. The man asked in a gentle voice, as if he were afraid that he might scare a blind man, if there was a Carl Gurley employed at the shop. Now Louis was no fool, possibly remembering people who asked questions like this from his lost weekends, and immediately said, "Well no friend, old Carl up and quit last week." The guy was no fool, and in that same gentle voice said "Well friend, if you do see him please give him these clothes," and with that he turned on his heels and left. After I checked to be sure the polite man was gone, Gurley crawled out of the fitting, as Louis fondled the bundle of clothes. With a knowing smile he asked Carl, "Caught you in bed with her, did he?" And Carl replied, "Hell no, I went out the back window as he came in the front door."

Poplar was still skid row, hardly changing from the first time I laid eyes on it. The down-and-outers were more likely to be just drunks, often mean, with not a touch of gentleness. I didn't like that, but I didn't want things to change either.

18

TWO KIDS GET MARRIED

On a cool, clear morning in the spring of 1950 Amelia and I were married. We had done all the customary things in proper order. Her father was lost in the background, so I asked Mrs. Solari for Amelia's hand in marriage. I went to Brodnax Jewelry to choose Amelia's ring. It was the place to go in Memphis for quality, and it was also the place to go for price because I was able to put the ring on lay-a-way and spread the payments over several months. Finally, just two weeks before the wedding I was able to get the ring out, paid in full. We also bought a bedroom suite from Rhodes, which I would pay for on time as well and pay off after we found an apartment. But before all that, there was the honeymoon.

Although we were teenagers, it seemed that we had known each forever. Yet there was the unknown. It was plain to all, we were just two young kids with no money. Still, there was a certain maturity about us, which no one questioned. We never wavered. We were meant for each other and would be stubborn as mules if challenged.

We married at Blessed Sacrament Catholic Church, the same church we had attended as children and the church where I first saw her. And we were married by the same priest who I served as an altar boy. Amelia was radiant. So pretty in her borrowed gown, she took my breath away. Her poise stunned me. She was composed. In contrast, I who had been the mature one in our twosome, was nervous and self-conscious. The whole event was too much like a dime store novel, but had a feeling of being just right.

There was a small reception at the Solari home after the ceremony. Everyone enjoyed toasting the new bride and groom. My dad and Mr. Solari along with Clyde and several other guests had too much to drink and acted a little foolish, but it was a celebration and was overlooked. Among all the guests, I was disappointed but not surprised to find that the men from the shop had not come. I suppose it was a blessing in some ways. The men were hard fellows who lacked experience in family customs or social traditions. Rituals of worship and ceremony were not part of the world in which they existed. Perhaps the men would be embarrassed, or maybe they feared embarrassing me. In all, they probably gave it little thought, just another day and the boss's kid getting hitched. For us, it was the beginning of life.

Our honeymoon started in style in a new Plymouth, which we borrowed from my Aunt Ruth because she insisted that we use it. She had just purchased it, and wouldn't take no for an answer. Aunt Ruth told Amelia, "Honey, I don't have a bit of use for it. I can walk to the corner and catch the bus straight to Saint Joseph Hospital." Dad had been reluctant when he offered the Desoto. The Desoto sounded as if the engine was going to fall out when it shifted gears, and Dad was uptight about it in general because he had gotten a raw deal when he bought it. Although, he would never admit that he had gotten stuck with it. And I was happy to take the Plymouth.

We drove the Plymouth down Highway 51 toward Jackson, Mississippi—honeymoon bound. We would be together for a whole week with plenty of time to get to know each other. No excuses. No interruptions. No reason for lack of intimacy. It was a sweet, embarrassing adventure. The windows were down, letting in dirt that gathered on our clothes, and grabbed our voices, making it impossible to talk unless we yelled. The gully washes were five feet deep on either side. No rain and they were empty. The landscape flew by along each side of us. We rode quietly for a long while, and Amelia slide my arm around her and pressed up against my side as we rolled along. The sun streamed across the windshield and thoughts of what lay ahead passed through our heads. Finally, tired of choking on dust and staring at the road, I stopped and rented a cabin at a roadside motel.

In a ring like a circle of wagons, amongst a dozen just like it, lay our very own pine cabin. Knotty pine boards and a fresh breeze filled the place as the fading sun filtered through lace curtains on the window at the head of the double bed conspicuously in the center of the small space. Across the room was a small table and two chairs and on another wall the doorway to a small bathroom. Alongside the door was a large chest of drawers and a suitcase rack. We unpacked, dragging each article of clothing from our bags piece by piece. Amelia laid her things neatly on the bed, and I rested my case on the rack and took my clothes and placed them in the top drawer of the chest. The suitcases I took and placed in a small alcove behind a heavy curtain, which passed for a closet, and hid the only clothing rack in the room. Amelia had already moved her things into the drawer under mine leaving the rod bare. Then I turned to her. Were we suddenly shy. The girl and boy who had known each other all their young lives. Nothing to say between the two of us who had talked endlessly about our future plans. Were we afraid?

We had been warned by the priest, the brothers and the nuns of the grievous sin of birth control. In this case there was no planning

120

just doing. Being a young Catholic couple meant wading unknown waters. There were tremendous implications, much of it we had barely begun to consider. Despite the warnings since well before our teens to avoid contraceptives, each of us had been warned more recently and more openly about the pitfall and impracticality of no birth control. Amelia's sister-in-law, Virginia, was flabbergasted at the thought that we should not plan our family. And all the men I worked with, though I considered them old-timers, had rather modern ideas about being prepared. They were surprisingly kind yet clear in their explanations. I knew what I could do. But we knew what we had been told was right.

At last, reasons to stay apart were gone. Amelia's shyness replaced the relaxed closeness we shared as we rode down the highway, my arm around her, my hand close to her side. As Amelia sat on the bed, the rigid shyness melted and tears ran down her cheeks. I was filled with doubt. I would reassure her, I reached to comfort her, and we fell together naturally, sweetly. No thoughts of fear or forbidding warnings of sinful acts. We were one. If my wife were to become pregnant from our first moment together then so be it. We were lost in each other. Hours passed and exhausted we fell asleep. The next morning was a brand new day, different but still the same. We were a bit sheepish at first, but soon hunger displaced the brief hesitation that acknowledged something deeper had transpired between us.

Hungry as hell, we were back on the road. A quick stop a café for breakfast, and we hit 51 again headed to New Orleans. It was the main highway taking us South cutting through the center of Mississippi. With our new found sense of freedom, we were soon craving more adventure and decided to take an auxiliary road marked for Gulfport. Neither one of us had seen the ocean, so we took this as our chance to head to the beach. Trying to ignore the potholes, we bobbled along the tree-lined path to the coast. After more than four hours, the Gulf appeared. I was the first to make out one of several ships floating on the horizon, which spanned as far as Amelia and I could see. It was like our new life together stretching out along time far beyond what the two of us could see. Forever.

Back on the street as we rode by, there were clip joints, an ice cream stand, shops and rides. Along the strip stood the Alamo Plaza Courts. It was a popular chain with units laid in the shape of its namesake. We took a room and would stay one night. As quickly as we could, we changed into our swim suits and eagerly hit the beach.

What we got was not what we expected. Even then when Amelia and I were young, the shores of Gulfport were a mix of darkened sand and pebbles, giving the appearance of being black. The waters were oily and tiny fish floated on the rippling tide that washed ashore. And the beach was covered with people. A mass of humanity spread across the sands with feet black from the sand, and many drinking beer. Some were already drunk and the rest were well on their way. Several couples were nearly to the point of making out with one another on blankets spread across the sooty-colored sand. Along the boardwalk, there were push-carts selling hot tamales and beer.

The crowds were noisy and gathered in number as the afternoon grew long. It was made up of mainly tough types with chubby, loud-mouthed girlfriends. It was the kind of crowd that could get rough quick. But it was such a glorious day that everyone was too busy enjoying themselves to get irritated by anyone else. As we wandered the beach for miles, Amelia and I splashed in the Gulf getting a lot of sun and finally finding a quite spot to rest along the way. As the sun began to drop low in the sky, we turned around and made our way back. It was a full day and had been a long night before it. We were weary when we reached our room. We showered and fell into bed. Shortly, Amelia began to feel sick at her stomach. Was this an omen? More likely, it was the greasy food we had eaten for lunch, which came right up. Amelia began to sob, fearing that she would ruin our honeymoon. Only when she continued to be sick through the following afternoon, did I consider what else could have made her so sick. My God I thought, "Do Catholics get pregnant on the first try?" I worried.

We left Gulfport a day later with Amelia sick as ever. For eighty miles, we drove until we reached New Orleans. There, we were in for a surprise. I had no idea things would be so expensive. We had a couple of days left and decided to budget and get by on the cheap to save up for a fancy dinner out in the French Quarter. We spent all our time there. We lapped up the music and even had a couple of drinks. When our last night in New Orleans came, I made reservations at the Court of Two Sisters, an elegant restaurant in the historic area. It was terribly expensive; everything on the menu was a la carte. Not only was the menu in French, there were no prices so I couldn't be sure that I was within the amount we budgeted for our fine meal out—a story to brag about when we returned home. It was our good fortune that the waiter was a seasoned, mature gent and noticed two kids dressed to the nines who weren't sure what to do next and offered his suggestions to smooth us through the awkwardness of our inexperience. In my coat and tie and Amelia in her favorite yellow dress, we ordered with the waiter's help. He helped us choose items that gave us a wonderful array of Creole foods to savor. At the time, it seemed like we were more dressed up than anybody else in the place, and it felt as though we were small town hicks out of place. But that was just because we were kids, and we were having a series of firsts as many young couples do. We were no more out of place or one thing or another than the rest of the people in the restaurant, only perhaps younger than most. We enjoyed each other and the delicious dishes delivered to our table. The room filled with people, but they all faded into the background. We were focused on one another.

As we finished, I watched the other men at other tables. I watched them leaving tips, all bills, on the table as they walked away. I wondered what to do as I received the bill for our meal. I knew I had just enough to cover it. There was only a quarter left. So I did the only thing that I could do; I left a quarter, the last of my money, for the tip. I learned many things during that week, about life, about myself, and about my wife. What a funny ring that word "wife" had at the time.

Amelia was practical and frugal; she was quick to check prices before making a selection after our meal in the French Quarter. During the short trip I learned that my wife would go out of her way to save a few cents, demonstrating her concern about our expenditures in relation to the hard work and hours I put in to earn a living. I learned that she could be as tenacious about things she was passionate about as she could be about economizing. At the time we didn't know it, but this would be our last trip for some years to come. One thing we were not short on was time, and even in the short time on our honeymoon had grown to know each other's temperaments, moody spells and how cranky we both were in the morning. In that one week, we had made the first step toward the rest of our lives.

19

THE ICE CRUSHER AND
A SON IS BORN

The apartment had a kitchen with linoleum flooring. The bedroom was barely large enough for our newly purchased furniture, and there was one bathroom, which we shared with the owner of the house. We found the place through a relative, and it was all we could afford. Originally, it had been a single-family home, but the house had been closed off on one side of the dining room to create a duplex. A hole had been knocked in the kitchen wall to make room for an outside entrance. There a doorway opened to a dinky concrete porch too small for even one chair. The place was neat and bright, filled with sunlight from numerous windows. Sharing the bathroom with the landlady was inconvenient to say the least, but it was what we could manage at $40 a month rent. She was an old widow, and was the most disagreeable person I've ever encountered. But the location was convenient on Snowden near Watkins, and I could walk just a block to the corner and meet Dad and Louis every morning for a ride to work.

Work hadn't changed any in the short time that Amelia and I were away. Each morning was just the same as before with the two of them yelling back and forth making plans for the day. Despite the fact that yelling was the standard form of communication between Dad and my uncle, their disputes had become more pronounced, and they were having a harder time coping with change. Like it or not Werner was going to have to do more than just gutters, flashing, and steeple work. I noticed for the first time that Louis seemed unsure of himself; Werner was now being underbid on slate work and tile roofing, the one trade that we could always fall back on. I saw this as an opportunity to speak up. After a week of holding my breath, I put in my two-cents worth and was surprised when they listened, agreed and kept quiet as they considered my suggestions. From then on, the day's plan was made by one red-faced, middle-aged man, one blind man yelling and one kid in the back seat timidly making suggestions as we rattled down the street for all the world to see.

I had followed through on my promise and spent my evenings pursuing additional education through correspondence courses. My evening routine went as follows: come home, wash up, eat quickly, then study. While Amelia sat on the back porch steps afraid to talk, I would study for hours. She knew I would bite her head off, so she left me to my studies even at times when we needed to discuss something important or she simply needed the company and conversation. There were times I didn't want to study. Those were mostly evenings when the afternoon car ride had not been a quiet one and the work had not gone well. Dad would have popped a couple of beers, and Louis would have milk curdling in his stomach wishing instead that it had been a few shots of whiskey warming his belly. On those days it was awfully hard to sit and study. But Amelia reminded me that we had saved our money for this school. Guilt ridden, I studied plans as she sat.

It took a couple of years to complete all my courses, but together we made it. I remember the special day a young man appeared at the office and asked for me. He was a representative from the school where I was taking my correspondence courses. He came into the shop and shook my hand and presented me with a certificate for the completion of my studies. I was thrilled. We were still poor as church mice, but I was of proud of my accomplishment. With the fifty-cent per hour raise I had been given, we were getting by and our prospects were getting better. It was all Dad could afford, but that was fine by me.

After rent, food, and necessities, there was little left over. By Thursday of each week, our cupboard was bare and Amelia would pull the same farce. She would call Mom, chat for a minute, and then ask, "What are you having for dinner, Nora?" And of course, we would be invited to dinner that night. Louie, who was attending Christian Brothers College, and Lee, who had graduated from Memphis State, both still lived at home and surely resented the intrusion but said nothing. Mom and Amelia had become a pair, and the family knew how close they had become. Mom brought Amelia out of her shyness. So instead of cleaning an apartment that didn't it or sitting by herself on the porch steps, Amelia would meet Mom at the bus stop and ride downtown, shop without buying anything, then have lunch at the counter of Bry's Department Store and come home. It was good for her and the closeness grew between the two of them.

We had spats like any newly married couple, and we were young and quite different from one another. Amelia couldn't boil water when we first married. She was different from my family in that she had always had her meals served to her. It was only those first few meals, late to the table because of a trip downtown and unpalatable because of no experience in the kitchen that were disasters. Within a month, Amelia had mastered the art of cooking roast beef and mash potatoes, which she could serve the next evening as hash to vary it up a bit. These two dishes were our staple dinner menu for months, and like nearly any man who worked hard all day, meat and potatoes was fine with me.

She was only eighteen and had left a life of contentment in which she had wanted for little. She left it to live in a small apartment, wash her husband's clothes by hand, and spend the majority of her day alone. She cooked for a man who walked through the door to eat immediately and then went off to study. It was not easy. But she did not complain. Still half asleep the next morning she would rise and once again begin preparing meals for the man she saw so little of. She would fix several sandwiches and fresh tea each morning, crushing ice inside a dishcloth by hand, breaking them against the concrete steps of the tiny porch to chill the tea in the Thermos.

Months of crushing ice went by. Then Amelia discovered a clever way to end pounding on the porch. For only $7.50, Amelia had found an ice crusher. No more mess. No more waking the neighbors. She put the gizmo on the wall and the next morning proudly chopped the ice into perfect sized cubes. I didn't notice the thing until she mentioned the price. Then, I was wide awake. At once, I told her to take the damned thing down and return it. Did she think money grew on trees? For the rest of the time that we lived in that duplex she crushed the old fashioned way, with a hammer against the steps of the porch.

Just when Amelia thought things were about to get better, the landlady roared into our lives. Amelia's mother had just given her a hand-cranked washing machine. It was complete with rollers and cranked at the top. Amelia could wash all the dirty clothes in a single morning. The next day our landlady raised our rent $5.00, assuming that we had experienced a windfall of some sort. She was determined to get her share.

On Sunday, all those petty issues were forgotten. Sunday was still our day—just the two of us. Amelia kept the glow of a newly married woman, and it showed in the way she walked the few blocks to Little Flower Church on Jackson Avenue. It felt good to dress up on our one day and go to church. Afterwards we'd go to the bakery and buy cinnamon rolls with icing on top. It was a dollar spent without fail every Sunday and worth every penny of it. Later, we might go to Whiteway Drug Store and get a soda or to the Rosemary Theater for a movie. Sometimes, we would just lay around and listen to radio serials. Soon we began walking to the Solari's because Al had installed a television set. It was the first we had seen, with a picture so small we had to huddle close around the set to see anything. Today, it would seem primitive, but it was so new to us it was a rare treat.

Six months later, we were on the horizon of the original and more complex of family traditions—pregnancy. What else could we expect? We had made our decision long before, and we treated the pregnancy like just another part of our life. It would have been nice to have a few more months to get to know each other or save money or discuss our plans further. There were concerns of where to put the crib, and hospitals and doctors and insurance, which we didn't have. However, there were plenty of odd jobs. I was working on Saturdays, sneaking into the shop on the sly. The business agent that Dad dealt with knew I didn't have a card, but Dad had convinced him that I owned part of the business. Fortunately, the agent had the good sense not to ask for proof. With the extra money, we could make it. The details would take care of themselves a day at a time, and we promised ourselves we wouldn't worry.

Things changed quickly when word got out that Amelia was pregnant. Virginia lowered the boom on me for being a young fool and not planning. The men at the shop took sides, and the ones with lots of brothers and sisters like Charley and Gurley thought it was great. Uncle Louis felt it was too soon and that Amelia and I needed more time alone as a couple. But any reservation we had washed away when our parents received the news. They were euphoric when they saw the look in our eyes. My mom and dad were especially elated since this would be the first grandchild.

Amelia grew and grew. She was healthy and had no complications or problems with the pregnancy. Then came the day in June, I left for work, and Amelia cleaned house. After a short time she felt liquid running down her leg. The doctor had instructed her that when the time came her water would break signaling that labor would begin soon, though that was not exactly what she had anticipated. But she had a doctor's appointment that very day and planned to ask about it then. She had a list of things she wanted to get done, which included paying our bill at Bry's. So she rode the bus downtown, stood in line and made the payment. Realizing that she was using the bathroom a lot and there wasn't time to do much else, she got back on the bus and rode to the doctor's office. There she waited patiently for an hour until her scheduled appointment. The doctor took one look at her and called me himself. Our son, Steve, was born some twelve hours later healthy, pink, and a brand new beginning for us.

20

DAD LOSES HIS BEST FRIEND

Eight months after Steve was born Louis died. It was awful. It was one of those things in life that were so unnecessary. For a week Dad and I rode to work, no yelling. Instead, Dad was grim-faced as he stopped at the corner each morning and then continued on, just the two of us. Uncle Louis had been hospitalized as a result of a simple stomach ache. His condition worsened until the poison in his system killed him. Acute peritonitis. It was the result of a ruptured appendix.

During the time that Louis was in the hospital, Dad and I would visit him every day. We would talk about work, how business was going, and that things were picking up. We talked about anything except Louis' condition and if he was improving. Ruth sat silently. Surely, she must have had contempt for the fool doctor who couldn't diagnose a case of appendicitis. All of it was to no avail. Louis was gone.

Dad had lost a brother, but more than that, he had lost a friend. Yelling and all, Dad would miss that man who helped him make the name Werner mean something in the construction business. I had lost the only real confidant I had. I mean the only one I could really trust. Louis told me more about adult life and sex than anyone else. He was honest and described things in frank terms without exaggerating. He helped me more than he knew. I remember the day he said, "JoJo, if you fool around with the wrong girl and you get her in trouble, you let me know. You hear?" He tossed it out casually as if the thought had just occurred to him, though I sensed he had been pondering on it for some time. And though I never had to take him up on any such an offer so grave, I knew he could help me with nearly any problem that I might encounter.

As we grew closer and Louis grew older, it made me sorry for the times as a youngster that I resented having to escort him on my arm. I would hate to have to guide him as he held my arm while we walked to Babe's Barber shop for his monthly haircut or to Sam's Grocery to get his quart of milk. I though he was a crank, telling far-fetched stories about his days as a rounder and constantly yelling and keeping Dad in an uproar. It took me a few years to learn what a good man he was and how important he was to me, to Dad and to the family.

Uncle Louis helped to build the foundation that made J. P. Werner Sheet Metal a solid concern in Memphis business. Dad and I would both miss Louis' keen mind for business problems and the way he would listen, screwing up his forehead into a hard frown as though the solution was rolling from one side to the other in his brain. I could almost see the numbers tabulating behind those sightless eyes. Then before Dad and I could put pencil to paper, he barked out a response that was the solution to our dilemma.

Business would go on, but it would be different. Mom would help Dad with our meager books, which still resided in a few folders on the roll top desk. I began to help with office duties as well. I went to the bank on Fridays for the amount of money needed to make payroll. No checks for these men. I placed cash in an envelope for each man with his name on it. I also kept up with my regular duties: working in the field, on roof tops and on steeples. When work was slower, I figured jobs and estimated by myself.

Although, business continued on a fairly regular way, I could only imagine how Aunt Ruth must have been getting through it. She was alone. Her whole life was devoted to caring for people and the one for whom she cared most was gone. Ruth remained in her position as head of nursing and continued to give her orders in the quietest of voices with the most angelic smile ever seen by the living. Dad made sure that he did right by her. He gave her an amount that he felt was proper, and I'm sure it was more than we could afford. But we managed not because it was written in a contract somewhere, but because we were family. More importantly, it was the right thing to do.

Like anything, there is a right and a wrong way to do things. Most of the time, I think we arrived at the right thing through a lot of trial and error. Work was like that a lot. With business picking up and the construction boom moving faster than the big shops could handle, I would wrangle a bid for a job sometimes by pure luck, arriving at a number that worked. One of the first bids I won was for a small church on Macon Road. It was a pretty church and a good project, but unfortunately once I got the job I didn't know what to do with it. Once I explained the problem to Dad his response was, "You got the damn job. Now, you do it."

I was working other things out in life on my own. Why should this be different? I would figure it out. But to my horror I learned that my bid had been far lower than anyone else's and I ran the risk of not making a dime on the deal. Once the crew stopped laughing, Gurley and Hank put their heads together and helped me make a plan We made the duct work. We borrowed equipment from other shops. We installed the system, and in the end we made a little profit. Together we created a decent outcome from an unreasonable situation. I thought Dad would be pleased for a change. But he was more difficult than I had expected. He just grunted unimpressed with our extraordinary efforts to save a job that was a near loss.

After our first taste of duct work, the Werner name was getting around town. Contractors would ask for us to come out and bid the jobs they wanted to get moving on quickly. Most of the jobs were too big, but work was plentiful now, and we could pick and choose. I was enthusiastic about the growing opportunities and would take sets of plans home to study and practice on. I would still use the hand crank adding machine and my slide rule. I learned how to pace myself and take a small job and then a medium job and make the business grow according to our capacity. Soon we had ten folders on the old roll top desk instead of four or five.

If things were getting a little better at Werner, the same wasn't happening at home. Amelia was pregnant again, but this time she had a miscarriage three months into it. There was no reason that the doctor could identify. And because of that, I think Amelia carried a lot of guilt. Solitude was her wonderful tool for recovery, and quietly, she dealt with it in her own time. Amelia could spend hours watching Steve play in the yard, never talking, always seemingly content. Most certainly the miscarriage bothered her as it bothered me, but youth has the benefit of adjusting quickly to most anything. Our life was full of good things, and we moved on.

I took great joy in looking out the screen door at my pretty wife and my sturdy young son. The sun shown on their faces and radiated from them with a brilliance that lit up my heart. I would leave my work on the kitchen table and walk outside, put an arm around each of them and feel the joy of youth and happiness. We had gone through a lot, but afternoons such as these would last a lifetime.

21

SAD TIMES

It was time to move on with our lives. We had outgrown the apartment on Snowden. We were tired of the overbearing landlady and not having enough room to swing a cat. Dad had given me a raise, and within a month I located a duplex on South Parkway, near Willett. It was set far back from the busy street with a huge front yard. The duplex certainly not as roomy or inviting as the homes around it, but ours was large enough and cheap enough to make us feel as if we could breath more freely. We wouldn't have to worry about the lady next door saying something sarcastic every time Steve cried. And even though our son would have to sleep in the kitchen, at least it was a bigger kitchen. It was an unusual area, a dinky duplex set among a nest of large homes, with a huge field that acted as a buffer from the railroad tracks. The tracks were used quite frequently by long slow trains with loud whistles making sleep at night a guessing game.

My cousin Walter moved into the opposite side of the duplex with his pregnant wife Caroline, one child, a huge gentle Great Dane named Tina, and a large turtle that wandered continuously from room to room. As children the Townsends had lived only four houses from us on Spring Street. Walter's mother Pauline was Mom's sister, so I had known Walter, who was Louie's age, all my life. As children, his brother, Charley, was the bully of the street, which came in handy on our way to Blessed Sacrament . His sister Mary was the baby of the family. My aunt seemed to always be in the background. I remember her as a smiling pretty lady who loved to dance, She was as devoted to Mom as Mom was to her. Uncle Joe was gregarious, loud, and one of the nicest people I ever knew. He had been a policeman and could often have the chore of bringing Grandpa home when he went on a toot. He quit the force because it frightened my aunt, but it thrilled us kids. Though he died at an early age, his memory lingers. Memories of Uncle Joe still bring a smile to my face.

With the move came a whole new life. Gone were the quiet days on Snowden. There were kids and dogs, and a turtle that kept getting lost, and the constant commotion of children. There was a yard for Steve to run in, and he could yell all he wanted without worrying about the lady next door. And there was a man who appeared every morning with a huge horse which he tethered in the empty field next to our house using a stake, which he pounded into the ground and attached to a long length of heavy chain. The horse was a constant menace as he pulled on the stake, stretching the chain taut, trying to get to more grass. Some late afternoons, when he had worked the stake loose and the whistle blew from a passing train, the frightened animal would tear across our front yard, barely missing the children. One day the horse finally broke loose and tore down Parkway, stake and chain in tow, never to be seen again.

On weekends our duplex became a gathering place. I had finally been able to buy a small television set and every Friday night a real "dukes mixture" of people showed up to watch the fights. Jim, who spent most of his career as a professor at Santa Clara, was always there and usually brought booze rather than beer. Ed, who became a lawyer and caring friend, always showed, as did Clyde and Walter. Louie came when he could get away from school. We would gather around the small set. People wandered in and out, usually drinking beer, arguing politics or books, and the fights in the background would be half forgotten. We ended the evening at the English Tavern, a dark, crowded beer joint on Lamar. It was a poor replacement for Alex's, the tavern on Jackson which had been our first love.

Amelia was pregnant again. She was twenty one and carrying her third child. She became lethargic, and even quieter than usual. She would sit on the steps and stare into space. Her complexion was pallid, and she gained more weight than she had during the previous pregnancies. Her ankles showed the water retention and swelled greatly. Surely none of it was a good sign.

I was busier than ever with Louis gone and tended to ignore her when I was home. I had my friends to run around with in the evenings. Amelia never complained, but, when asked, she said something didn't feel right even though the doctor told us everything was fine. She told me this baby didn't feel like Steve had, but I was too much of a fool to listen. The night came when she went into labor. We gave our son to Caroline to mind and drove to St. Joseph Hospital.

It was late at night so I called no one and sat in the waiting room, feeling lonely. I wanted to be alone. After six hours of hard labor Amelia delivered Constance, a six pound baby girl, and a birth that changed our lives forever. Amelia had bled much more than she should, which worried the nurse who made a constant check, watching for any change as I sat next to her bed and half slept . She looked peaceful in her hospital gown, and with no make up on her ashen face she looked as if she were fourteen rather than twenty one.

Although it was still not dawn the head nurse came into the room, touching Amelia's forehead with a wet cloth and quietly informed us there was a problem with the baby. The pediatrician, Dr. Arnoult, had been called. Asking what the difficulty was did no good. In the fifties the only person to explain medicine to patients were the doctors. Those Godlike creatures decided when and if the patient needed information, and how much information was to be dispensed, whether it be about their own body or one of their loved ones.

Within minutes Dr. Arnoult arrived. He fit no mold of any doctor we had known. He was a warm, caring man. He knew how to explain things without talking down to us. After a small hesitation he said, "There is a problem with the baby's blood. She will have to go through a procedure, a type of transfusion to change her blood." This brought up a thousand questions, but the only one Amelia wanted answered was, "Will our baby live?" The only answer Dr. Arnoult could give us was, "There's a chance if we do it immediately." I had called no one, not wanting to worry our families. I noticed that the nuns, even the head nun for the floor, began to stay away from our area. Amelia begged a reluctant Dr. Arnoult to bring the baby, and shortly he arrived with Constance in his arms. She held the baby for just one moment, and then he asked me to accompany him.

The two of us got on the elevator, and as the car rose he looked down, then back at me, with eyes so sad that I knew. He said, "Joe, your baby is dead." The first thing I felt was confusion. The baby seemed normal, healthy in fact, only as if she were sleeping. Yet she was gone. As Dr. Arnoult took the baby I rushed back and told Amelia, and the two of us broke down. I laid across the bed and held her until we finally slept for a short while. A child had died and no one came to offer solace. The nuns and nurses shunned us. They stayed at the end of the corridor until the family arrived. Dad was mad at the doctors, Mr. Solari was grimed faced, and we were kids again, leaning on Mom, Mrs. Solari, and Virginia.

It was one those awful things that never should have happened. Within a week Amelia's doctor called and asked that the two us come in for a consultation. He described in detail, speaking directly to me, as if my wife were not in the room, that Amelia had RH negative blood. My first thought was that she had some sort of disease. This was not the case at all, but since I had RH positive our red and white blood cells were not compatible. Speaking to me as if I was a child he explained that the result was her cells, over a period of months, built up antibodies which killed out my red cells. The only chance a baby would have was to change the blood immediately after birth. When I then asked why this was not done with Constance he put on his sternest "doctor" face and said, "You need to understand that people make mistakes. I'm afraid the lab registered your wife's blood as RH positive." He then leaned back in his swivel chair, folded his hands over his round little stomach, and stared at me as if to dismiss us. I was so furious I was shaking. I wanted to go across the desk and smash that complacent face. Instead I looked at Amelia, sitting with her head down, her hands in her lap, tears running down her face, and my only thought was to get her out of that awful place. We got in our old car. I was shaking too much to drive. Then my wife reached across and held me, and I knew there was nothing that could ever come between us and that the pain we suffered had only made our love stronger.

After Steve was asleep that night we talked and decided to call Dr. Arnoult, who we now considered a friend, and he graciously invited us to his home. After the usual small talk he explained, "I'm sorry, there's no easy way to say this. Steve was born because the first baby is never affected by the RH factor, but with each succeeding birth the risk becomes greater that the baby will die, even if the blood is changed." We talked for a long while that night, trying to understand, to grasp any straw that Dr. Arnoult offered, no matter how remote. When we left the doctor's home I dropped Amelia off, telling her I needed to do some work, but what I did was to go to visit a priest. Since we had first known each other Amelia had put her trust in me to make the decisions, and so far I had done a damned poor job. It was my decision to not use birth control—something she had never questioned— and now, there was probably only a small chance that we could have another healthy baby.

The rectory was empty, so I went into the church and knelt. Guilt washed over me, knowing that every time my wife got pregnant we were risking her life. Yet, kneeling with no one in the church but me, and even though no saint came down to touch my shoulder, nor did God speak to me from the heavens, I knew in my heart that we were going to someday have another baby. When I arrived home Amelia was waiting, surely knowing where I had been, and why. As I explained how I felt she only nodded and said, " Joe, that's up to you." With that simple sentence my guilt was complete.

22

THE PARADE—A LAST HURRAH

The Korean War was coming to an end, and Memphis' skid row was taking a different shape. The old buildings from years before were just as dank and depressing, the walls still dark with soot, reminding one of dried blood. The usual down-at-the heel types were as much familiar to us as the sweet-sour odor of the area. But now there was a new crowd coming on the scene, a numerous bunch of younger and more aggressive characters descended on the area like a flock of buzzards. The street began to attract every down-and-outer, wino, and thug like road kill on a hot summer day. The sidewalk was jammed with the new carrion picking the bones of the old regulars and leaving them discarded in the gutter.

A few months before, a young man had moved into a small building at the corner of High Street and Poplar, and named it Memphis Union Mission. The Mission welcomed anyone who needed a bed and a meal. The only stipulation was the usual ritual of a little preaching and reading of the bible before the meal which was a small price to pay for the benefits received. However, the effect on Poplar was disastrous, and the street was overrun with a new breed of deadbeat.

As in everything on skid row, when discreet force was needed, Abie came to the rescue calming troubled waters in a matter of days. With the help of his connections in the police department, thugs began disappearing from the street and the laggards gradually disappeared. In the future the Mission would develop into a much needed lifeline for many, but to those of us who had spent so much of our lives there the street was beginning to loose its character.

Despite all the uncertainty, but mainly because Dad was becoming tired of me being under foot, we added a new office to the lime covered cubicle for my use. I was still operating as a combination sheet metal worker and estimator, and I needed a work area of my own. The place stretched pass the plate glass window, and I had plenty of room to stretch out to do my work. It was a larger room, built of two by fours, with a drop in ceiling and lined with the cheapest paneling we could find. My only luxury was a beautiful old desk that Mom found, one that had probably been in use for fifty years and would be for fifty more. Of course there was no sound proofing for privacy or concentration, but I felt like a real contractor with a set of plans spread out on the old desk, slide rule and hand-cranked adding machine at the ready. I was a professional even if the heat from the window made me sweat so badly I soaked the plans. I was moving up even though the noise from the shop deafened me. I would sometimes stop and lean back in my old swivel chair, look out the plate glass, and smile as I waved at one of the locals, who gave the thumbs up as if to say, "Way to go JoJo." Even Abie, who hated to see Dad get ahead of him in anything, could be seen with a set of plans in his hands as he ran across the street asking me to figure a job for him. Abie, like Dad, had never learned to read blueprints. I was having the most fun that I'd had in years. It felt good to have a little respect for a change.

I could hold my head high with things perking up in business and at home. Amelia was becoming herself again after the loss of our baby. She was more outgoing, less protective of Steve. I was making a little more money and spending more time figuring work instead of doing it. We were able to buy a car, a 1948 Ford coupe. It had no back seat, but it was far cry from " ole yeller," which was the shop's rattle trap. The Ford was much easier to sit in and less likely to bounce a passenger's head against the roof. After I bought the car, every Saturday was spent picking over the used parts in junkyards, searching for a back seat that would fit. We finally found one in an old Studebaker that would work. It didn't fit perfectly, but it would do. And with enough pillows lining the back seat, it did the job. Of course, as I had done for years, I picked up Cal every workday morning. He was always ready when I arrived and always quick to give opinions on the way I operated an automobile even though he had no driving license. But it didn't matter, because giving Cal a ride to work was a routine part of my workweek that I never minded.

Friday nights had become a ritual of sorts. Amelia and I with little Steve, who was becoming a chunky kid, would go to Robilio's Cafeteria on Vance and eat dinner before the guys came over to watch the fights and argue. Since the food was, at best, barely warm and the vegetables soggy, we went for the obvious reasons. The prices were cheap, and being Friday, like all Catholics they served fish. Money was still hard to come by since I continued to pay off doctor and hospital bills, but our life seemed to be settling into nice rhythm.

We regarded Sundays as the day for the three of us. For that reason I dreaded telling Amelia that I would have to work on a Sunday. It happened far too often. Churches were being built faster than filling stations and with each new church came a corner stone, and each corner stone had a copper box to hold the papers and artifacts. Soldering the top on the copper box, after the minister had blessed the various items, was normally an easy task. But with some two hundred pairs of eyes looking on with fixed gazes, it made for a nervous few minutes. Those Sundays were the only time when Amelia raised her voice. Even when I tried to explain that none of the men would be in good enough shape after a Saturday night to show up, much less be steady enough to solder, she made her displeasure with me plain. Finally church building slowed to a trickle, though filling stations didn't. Thank God filling stations didn't have corner stones.

Unfortunately, God didn't directly intervene in every aspect of business. The goddamned new union, as Dad called it, was a pitiful replacement for the fair minded bunch who I had known as a youngster. After some time, the new union bit off more than they could chew and got a taste of the will of the men they claimed to represent. As Labor Day approached the union sent to the shops, in a bold proclamation, that sheet metal workers could not participate in the annual parade down Main Street. The union stated the reason in unequivocal terms; in the past sheet metal workers had been an embarrassment. My dad and all the men at the shop were up in arms. How dare that bunch of scallywags ruin the most fun that they had every year. There was such a revolt the order was rescinded and the men had their day.

Most everyone put together something to create an outlandish costume for the parade. I made a tall hat with a wide brim. Cal made bottoms for his shoes which sounded like golf cleats on the concrete pavement while he did a little jig down the street. Hank made a banjo , which produced a tinny sound as he strummed out a tune. But Gurley outdid them all. His prop was a custom made walking-stick, soldered water tight, with a plug at the top. The hollow tube of the walking stick was capable of holding over a quart of whiskey. As the parade started at the end of Vance and Main Streets, the men were frisked by the union bosses for any hidden pints. Determined not to have a repeat of shenanigans as in previous years, alcohol was strictly forbidden. It seemed as we sauntered along, me in my Uncle Sam hat, that Gurley was a little wobbly by the time we reached Beale St. And after a few more blocks, even though the goons were keeping a sharp eye, our entire crew and many from other shops were wandering all over the street, whistling at girls and doing a strange hop, as if they were hearing a mambo that no one but they could hear. The entire bunch was basically smashed. When the parade reached the grandstand at Court Square the union bosses were raising their voices, cursing the whole bunch who were by now in complete disarray and having the time of their life.

That parade was a last hurrah for the old-timers of the union. After throwing the business agent out and installing one of their own, the dissension between the shop owners and the union became worse in a matter of months. The new agent was a talker, not a doer. He would instigate some sort of movement, have no idea where it was going, then back off when confronted. Al wasn't a bad guy, but he was in over his head, and within a year there was talk of a strike. Union meetings were two hours of threats, and finger pointing. By then the hard nosed union men were starting to check up on Al. They'd drive by his home each morning to see if his truck was still in the driveway at ten o'clock. If it was they'd go to the meeting and accuse him of being a drunk, which he wasn't, and lazy, which he was.

Buck saved the union from disgrace. He had come to work at Werner's, having moved from Seattle to Memphis because of arthritis and because of the constant gloom and rain in the Northwest. He was thin as a garden post, stronger than he looked, and had hands so gnarled they made one cringe. Buck did everything at a slower pace than the other shop men. He moved almost in slow motion, but made every move count, and at the end of the day would turn out more fittings than most and he never complained about the working conditions. One rainy day Buck and I worked on the brake all morning. We pulled the lever down, then lifted it to bend the metal. It was a grueling task. Buck didn't say a word the entire time, just hung in there with me pulling and lifting. But when the break came for lunch I noticed tears of pain streaming down his cheeks. Buck was a good family man and all his life had been a good union man. When it was obvious that a level head was needed to right the floundering union, Buck ran and won. He beat Al in a landslide. Within a few months the union was running on the straight and narrow.

Buck was the sort that talked sense to the bosses and the men, even the hard nosed ones. However, as in everything involving large groups of men, within a few years complacency set in. A bunch of trouble makers decided to run a younger guy, one of the studs, who promised better wages, more break time, and even used the magic word "strike."

Buck lost in a landslide. Kicked out. He had been honest, hard working, and didn't threaten strike with every other breath. His arthritis soon got the best of him. He spent his last days in a wheel chair, living on a small pension. It wasn't much of a wheel chair, just enough for him to roam from room to room in his small home. There had been a half hearted attempt to raise money through the union members to purchase a motorized wheel chair, but it all came to nothing. When I heard of what had happened some time later, I thought of what good union men Dad and all of the old-timers had been and could only shake my head in sadness and frustration.

23

A TORNADO AND THE THE MISERIES

Dad had hired Squat because of Abie. On a Monday morning, the one day of the week when he never planned ahead, he leaned back from his roll top desk and looked across the street as two men hooked up a portable welding machine to the rear bumper of a pick-up truck. Dad hollered at me in my so called office, "JoJo, Art's been taking that God damned machine out on a job every day for a year. There must be money in laying decking, or Abie wouldn't be messing with it." And just like that we were in the decking business.

Metal deck had taken the place of wood sheathing. It was cheaper and easier to install. Each sheet was two feet wide and twenty feet long, prefabricated, with grooves every six inches. The part Dad liked best was its simplicity. All it took was a portable welding machine, two guys with strong backs to lay the decking in place and a "stick man" to weld the deck to the bar joist.

Squat was the perfect man for the job. He had come to work for Werner shortly after the Korean War. He was a little fellow, no more than five six and one hundred and thirty pounds, soaking wet. Squat was his given name. It was put on him at birth by his mama at the time when she lived in Texas and fell for a bronco buster at the rodeo, or so he said. He always looked spiffy in his jeans and shirt, both in black, with pearl snaps and shiny cowboy boots with silver taps. The gimmie cap he wore on the back of his head was almost like an afterthought. As a tinner he was no better than a member of a bull gang, but give him a welding machine and a seam to weld and he was a wizard. Soon, Art and his crew were watching each morning from across the street as Squat and a couple of men loaded the truck and headed out to another job Dad had picked off from one of his friends.

Good things just never seem to last long. Through an old friend, Dad had come up with a job at National Distillers. They needed a tunnel large enough for a man to walk in, made of heavy gauge metal, with solid welded seams. It would have a conveyor attached to the roof to move whiskey casks from one area to another, where they would be filled and set for aging. When we got the job we were in hog heaven, with Dad even suggesting that we sit down and have a beer together. We knew that in Squat we had the best welder in town, and with a good bull gang the job seemed to be right down our alley.

The tunnel progressed well, and as it neared completion and Squat was running out of seams to weld, Dad landed another decking job. It was a huge warehouse in Whitehaven. It was a storage building covering four acres, a perfect fit for Squat and a couple of good men. That afternoon Dad and I sat down to celebrate again with a beer, something I thought I might get used to, when the phone rang. Squat was in the emergency room in serious condition. He had been welding a seam, an arm hanging over each side of a tee bar for support when the welding machine shorted out. Squat probably would have been a dead man, being slowly burned to death if Rub, an ex-ranger just out of the army and newly hired, didn't have the nerve and strength to run full bore and knock Squat away from the metal. Though he would live, Squat was burned so badly it took months for him to heal. He fully recovered and worked for years to come, but always had an awkward way of holding his arms away from his body after having both armpits burned so badly that the muscle had collapsed.

Rub turned out to be a Godsend. He was another cousin, and one that Dad had qualms about hiring. His reputation preceded him, but Dad was never a man to turn kinfolk away. He was a strong young man, two years older than me, who had been a ranger in the army for four years. After being discharged he knew little of civilian life, but needed to find a trade. He was long and rangy, with muscles that looked like rope, handsome in a rugged sort of way, and teeth so white they looked false. Rub was a throwback to the old days, often telling me, "JoJo, I shouldn't drink because I get mean." But did anyway. He was never a top notch mechanic and often lost his patience trying to become a shop man. Layout work just wasn't his style, his work was far too rough, and he couldn't read a set of plans worth a damn. But he could out work anyone in the shop and run a bull gang better than most, always making Dad money. Rub stuck with Werner for many years, running big jobs both in town and out of town. Sometimes he ended up in scrapes, but it was never anything too serious. Then one day he got itchy feet, and moved to Alaska to work on the pipe line.

I went home that evening with the knowledge that I would be the welder for the decking job, and with it came a sinking feeling. I knew it would take me away from being an estimator, the job that had begun to fit like a glove.

It had been a hell of a day, and when I got home it didn't get any better. Caroline, who was pregnant again, sat with Amelia, both in lawn chairs while her two young ones ran around the front yard with Steve. She leaned over, talking in that quiet, soothing voice of hers, while Amelia sat collapsed into herself, as tears streamed down her face. I sat in the car for a few minutes, trying not to lose my temper, simply mad at the world. When I approached Amelia quietly told me, "Joe, I'm pregnant." My stomach began to hurt as it had for months. I lashed out at my wife, "What the hell do you want me to do about it?" I went into the house and got a stiff drink, then another, then walked next door and had a drink with Walter. Then I called Jim, picked him up and the three of us went to the English Tavern where we got good and drunk.

It was one the most cowardly things that I could have done, and I paid for it the next day. I got up feeling awful with both guilt and a hangover, my stomach hurting again and the first words Amelia said were, "I'm sorry" and put her arms around me, somehow knowing the way I felt. It was the first time since our marriage that I felt helpless, the first time that I felt lost. We talked. This time Amelia was the one who was doing the reassuring. She was telling me we were going to have a fine, healthy baby. While our son slept we made love, then held each other until Steve woke. We put our son between us, and for a little while we forgot about hospital bills, the car notes, and work that didn't pay enough. We only felt the warm sun—which always felt better on a Saturday morning—and knew that somehow, no matter what lay ahead, everything would be just the way we dreamed when we were first married.

We started the Penny job on a Monday morning at the beginning of June. Contractors never began a job on Friday, as it was considered bad luck. There were three of us. I was the "stick" man. Rub and Junior were to lay the decking. Junior was a new kid straight from the farm, green as new grass, but a willing worker starting his first day on the job. Junior had an abundance of freckles, lots of curly red hair, and like most country boys took long, high steps, as if he were walking through rows of cotton. Rub took one look at the roof we had to deck and said, "My God." From Junior's expression it seemed that he might be wishing he were back on the farm, with nothing to do but hoe the cotton.

For the next two months it was just the three of us. Every morning we would climb the ladder, Rub and Junior would scatter the decking out, fitting the grooves together, and I would make the weld. Eight hours a day that summer I would begin the by tying on a leather apron to protect my clothes from sparks, don the welding helmet, and, like Rub and Junior, pull on high flanged cotton gloves. Then while they lay the decking I would pull the helmet down, make a spot weld from deck to bar joist, raise the helmet, move two feet, and repeat the process, while all the time dragging a half inch cable behind me like a two hundred foot snake. I breathed the acrid smoke each time I made a weld. It was tiresome, monotonous work, and tempers became short. We would have little spats, and forget why we had them. We would stop often to drink a cup of water, then pour some over our heads. After a hard day's work, the three of us would pause and look back to see how little we had done and how many acres we had to go, except maybe for Junior who was probably thinking of how the cotton field didn't sound so bad after all. The work was so repetitious, one would forget the little things that could do harm. Every few weeks I would start a weld before pulling the helmet in place, and the spark would create a "flash" which immediately caused intense pain to the eyes. The pain was quick and I'd lose my vision. On those few occasions, Rub would lead me to the ladder and drive me home. There I would do the one thing that cured the flash, at least according to experts like Squat. I would put flax seed in the infected eye, cut a raw potato into slices, place it over my eye, lay back on the bed, then wait for the pain to cease. The cure sounded like an old wives tale, but by the next morning the pain would be gone, and I would be back on the job. Then after a while I would forget, get careless, and do the same stupid thing.

It was on a terrible, hot day in July that I was almost killed. We had been making good progress, even stopping too rest and look back in wonder at the huge expanse of steel. Heat waves rose from the metal, distorting the view. There wasn't a cloud in the sky, not a whisper of a breeze. It felt far too still. The three of us stood quietly, when, for some strange reason Rub said, "I don't like the feel of it," and looked at Junior. The ex- farm boy began to bob his curly red head up and down pointing to the horizon, "That mess of clouds yonder is about to bring up a hell of a storm, if not a tornado." The wind began picking up the loose decking, making a rattling sound like a drunk when the bottle hits his teeth as he takes his first drink of the day. When I looked around there were only the three of us. All the other trades had gone for the day, waiting for us to finish the roof so they could begin their work. I started gathering up the welding cable, when Rub hollered, "Screw that stuff JoJo, the storms already here." Within minutes the raindrops were coming down, as big as quarters, and before we could even start for the end of the building where the ladder was located we were drenched. Rub quickly became our leader, the ex-ranger in him taking over, leading the way, running across rain slick bar joists, only four inches wide to a column some thirty feet away. We slid down the column not thinking, just following the leader, and when we hit the ground Rub ran for a deep culvert in the distance. We lay huddled in the ditch, the pieces of decking flying overhead like whirly birds stabbing the ground like sharp knives cutting through warm butter. The storm lasted only minutes, but to the three of us it lasted a lifetime. Rub was the real man that day, those years of training paid off. He knew what to do and he did it. We packed up our equipment and left, steel strewn on the ground, decking everywhere. But we cared little. We were just happy to be alive. No one spoke except Junior, who proclaimed that this had been the most excitement he'd had since leaving the farm.

But my day had just begun. When I parked in the driveway that afternoon, completely exhausted, my car was only one of many. Mom, Dad, the Solaris, and Walter and Caroline were all in our home. Amelia was sitting in the small living room still as Lot's wife, and I knew even before Walter said anything that our baby was dead. The room was quiet, waiting for me to explode, handling things like my dad, lashing out at something or someone. But this day I had gone through too much. I left the friends and family and walked to the bathroom and threw up, leaning over the toilet thinking, no more, no more. I will not kill the one person that I love more than life itself. We've got each other, and a beautiful son. Why not leave it at that? So I sat while Amelia described how the doctor had told her that our baby was dead in her womb, but she would need to carry it full term and deliver the infant as if were a living thing. I saw the horror in her eyes, and in the eyes of everyone in the room until someone blurted out, "You mean you have to carry a dead thing in your stomach for another month?"

The small room was stifling; the window fan working overtime. I looked over and saw Steve sitting in a corner looking at his mother. She had a pained expression she was trying to hide. I thought about all the pain he must have seen on her face since he was a baby. I picked him up and held him tight, wanting him to know how much I loved him, wanting it to be just the three of us.

Gradually the house emptied, everyone uncomfortable, and for the second time in a month it was Amelia who did the reassuring, "Don't worry Joe, the doctor said everything is normal. It will be an easy birth." I knew then that this wisp of a girl who I had fallen in love with had more inner strength than me.

The time flew, Amelia's stomach grew no bigger and we never mentioned it. I never told her about the wind storm, and how close I had come to death. The three of us shunned others, and clung together waiting. One night Amelia went into labor and I called no one, only asking Carolyn to watch over Steve. Walter wanted to come and sit with me, but I refused. It only took a short while. Amelia delivered the dead infant, went to the recovery room, and soon she and I were together. The time would come when decisions had to be made, but for now I sat and held the hand of my wife. When the nun came into the room and insisted I leave so that Amelia could sleep, I held my her one more time then left, still calling no one. The exhaustion of the day swept over me, my mind became a blur.

I drove though the streets, quiet as a graveyard, finally stopping in a park by the river. In the past months I had come within a whisker of being killed and somehow been spared, yet my wife delivered a baby that would never see the light of day. I was so terribly confused. Nothing was working out the way that we had dreamed just a few years ago. As I sat in that park, I thought, "I'm twenty-four years old.

I have a wife that trusts me to make the proper decisions, and so far in four years of marriage, I've endangered my wife, we've had four babies, and only one lived." I felt discouraged, and lost, and for the first time, I didn't know where to turn.

24

DAD'S BEER COOLER
THE MOONSHINERS
AND THE LEAKY STEEPLE

It took a long time for Amelia to recover her strength in both body and spirit. For months I would come home from work and she would still be in her nightgown watching some children's program on the tiny television screen, Steve in her arms. I wanted to tell her that things were going better at work, that before long I might quit wearing jeans to the shop every day, but she showed no interest even when I got a nice raise, one that would help pay off the mountain of bills that we had accumulated over the last year. Hospitals and doctors were dunning us with nasty notes making my stomach cramp constantly. Finally I would lose my temper and blow up, my answer to everything, and Steve would look wide eyed while his mother began to cry and go into the bedroom. In desperation I called the one

I trusted most , Dr. Arnoult, and asked him to talk with us. Within an hour he had convinced Amelia that her depression was the most natural thing in the world. She had been raised since childhood that anyone in authority—doctors, priests, nuns—were both feared and obeyed without question. Yet this kind man, with his gentle manner, convinced her that she had no reason to feel guilt and soon had her smiling for the first time in weeks. Within a few days I came home one afternoon and there was my wife in her best dress and a son dressed to the nines waiting at the door and saying, "Joe, I want us to go out to eat at someplace special tonight, and it had better not be Rebellio's." Once again we had crossed another bump in the road, maybe a bigger one than usual.

Whatever guilt I felt about the situation at home had to be set aside when I arrived at the shop. Dad was taking a well deserved back seat, his arthritis had become worse over the years, and constant work and worry had taken their toll. Dad was tired and just wanted to hang it up and relax. I did most of the estimating on installing duct work, something Dad still despised, and he would spend the day riding the jobs with me. It was more for the pleasure of the ride than to stop and look at the square concrete and glass buildings, with not a slate roof or copper gutter in sight. Most of the crew were newcomers, Dad hardly knew their names, and were younger and not as outgoing. But they respected Dad, and always addressed him as Mister Joe. The new crew followed the union contract as if it were the bible, taking their break each morning and afternoon, and would stop in the middle of bending a piece of metal if the clock struck four- thirty. They weren't bad guys, most were good family men, worked hard, and gave a man eight hours a day, but don't ask for an extra half hour as that was against union rules. There was loyalty, but it was to the union and not to the shop they worked for.

Hell would freeze over before Dad let go of one custom. Directly outside the lime colored office attached to the door frame was a square box made of heavy gauge sheet metal lined with insulation that had copper piping coiled on the bottom. Every morning the apprentice with the least seniority was sent to the nearby ice house to procure a twenty five pound slab of ice which was placed in the cooler atop the coils. The end result was a tap which produced the coldest water in town, and also served as a resting place for the quart or two of Jax beer that Dad drank every afternoon. At exactly four thirty Dad reached into the cooler, a signal that it was quitting time, and open his beer on the bottle opener attached to the same door frame, just below the spot blackened by Louis's matches from years before. He would lean against the cooler and drink his quart of beer, his belly hanging over his trousers, just as Louis had done before him drinking his quart of milk. It was a perfect throwback to the old days, one that seemed to fit in just as Louis had with his quart of milk.

There were still steeples to be covered, but damned few of them. The churches had become monoliths amid the new school and office buildings. As one drove around town all the structures looked the same; gone were those beautiful buildings with slate roofs and fancy copper work such as Southwestern College and Idlewild Church. Once in a while a church with a steeple would come along and Werner would get the job, almost by default. The last church with a shop made steeple, prior to the manufactured type, was on Union Avenue extended. They had a small congregation that couldn't support the upkeep, and was eventually torn down. It was designed by an incompetent architect and built by a contractor who normally built homes. The construction for the framework of the steeple was shoddy; the steel work swayed back and forth with a high wind. Charley would somehow have made the copper watertight but couldn't do the work as he had been in the hospital for weeks, hit by a falling hammer which punctured a hole in his stomach. Louie, who worked part time while he was going to college, had been standing just a few feet from Charley when he was hit and was lucky the sledge hadn't hit him, having just moved from the spot where it fell. Louie must have been shaking since the normally stoic Charley was screaming in pain. He had somehow gotten Charley down from the roof and driven him to the emergency room, but the torn stomach muscles kept him off work for the entire summer. The only replacement was Len, one of the new men and a fairly good shop man, said he had done steeple work before, which was probably a lie.

Len was no more than five feet six, had a nose that was bent worse than mine, an irregularity in his back large enough to make him look hunchbacked, and a mountain twang so thick one could understand only a few words of each sentence he spoke. But at least we knew he could work with copper having come from the hills of Tennessee where he had grown up building stills made of copper for moonshine whiskey. Dad was quick to start a discussion with Len about the stills, about their capacity, what the configuration was like, and how long it took to build one. Dad had probably made more money at night and on weekends during prohibition than any other time in his life. Dad had Smith Sheet Metal Supply, located on North Main, keep a stock of copper hidden away in the back of their warehouse for easy access. There was a good chance that Revenue Agents would waltz into Smiths at any time and search for the copper. When there was a still to be made Dad would take the old truck at a prearranged time after dark, bring the material back to the shop and work late into the early morning hours building the still, then hiding the pieces until that weekend. Late on Friday night he would load up the pieces of copper, charcoal and a soldering outfit, then follow the moonshiners into the wolf river bottoms, to a place only God could find. He might work most all night but when finished he would be paid handsomely in cash on the spot then head home, knowing he had no worry about agents since their week ended at four on Friday. It was a sad day in the Werner household when the prohibition law was lifted.

Jackson was to be Len's helper. He was a huge man and a veteran of the Korean War with no experience in sheet metal work. He had a nasty disposition, possibly because he had a knot in the middle of his forehead as big as a walnut which he was very touchy about. He tried to grow bangs to hide the knot, but was unsuccessful since his hair was beginning to recede. He did have one positive attribute, he wasn't afraid of heights. I had checked the job as it progressed, but had never been able to get the architect or contractor to climb the scaffold in order to show them the shoddy workmanship of their crew. The job was complete, the scaffold had been removed, and the church was ready to be occupied. Then on a rainy, windy Friday afternoon the superintendent called and complained that the steeple was leaking. There were opening services to be held on Sunday, and water was ruining the new plaster ceiling. Dad just looked at me. Both of us knew that Len and Jackson were on the job, so there must be a reason they weren't trying to fix the leaks. When I looked out the window at the rain and the wind picking up I pretty well knew why, saying "I'll go on out there and check on it." Dad starting yelling, "Let the son of a bitch leak. They should have built it right in the first place." Dad knew as well as I did that there was probably some shoddy workmanship to go along with the poor steel construction. Finally with no decision reached between the two of us, I drove to the job, not yet scared, but knowing that I would find the two just as I thought I would, standing on the ground and staring at the sky. Len was shaking his head and Jackson rubbing his knot. I did my best to think like Charley and finally said, "Can't we just chalk the joints where the cross meets the plate on top?" Len stared at me like I was crazy, saying not a word, but Jackson said, "Screw it. I ain't climbing that thing in this rain." I never knew whether I was trying to prove myself to this new crew or in my mind to prove to Charley that I was still a steeple jack. Whatever the reason, the three of us climbed to the crest, sat the extension ladder across the ridge and while Len and Jackson held the ladder I climbed to the top, wiped the joint dry with the drop cloth and tried to chalk the seams watertight. After slipping a couple of times and getting nowhere in making the joint tight I decided that Jackson wasn't such a fool after all, and slid the last few feet down the ladder. When we finally hit the ground, the two of them took off like scalded dogs to buy a pint, figuring they had earned it. I drove back to the shop, wet as a mud hen and shaking like a leaf, knowing that I had done something very dangerous and very foolish When I got back to the shop it was dark, the wind and rain had increased and everyone but Dad was gone. I was still shaky and Dad was as mad as I had ever seen him. It was another mistake I had made that day in not realizing how helpless he must have felt sitting in the dark all alone wondering what in the hell I was up to.

That stunt took the wind out of my sails, but Dad and I talked more like adults after that. Louie was working part time while he began college at Christian Brothers, destined to become the inside man just as uncle Louis had been many years before. Dad, who was enjoying his rides more each day with no worries now, would talk as the two of us drove the jobs. We spoke about how it all started with Grandpa, then became Dad and Louis, and now Louie and me. For the first time in my life I hadbecome comfortable with my father. No more bristling the minute we started a discussion, and having Louie in the office seemed to help. Dad was no good at collecting from slow paying contractors, and I was in the poor position of asking for money while at the same time trying to get a contract. But Louie had the perfect philosophy: if we did the job, then we expected o be paid on time. It was a pretty neat arrangement, even thogh a bit crowded. But as usual, things were about to change

25

THE MAN IN A BLACK HAT COMES TO SKID ROW AND THE HIGH STEPPERS LEAVE

Skid Row was coming apart piece by piece, beginning to crumble just a little at a time. Babe's Barber Shop had closed, the place where I had taken Louis years ago to have his once a month haircut. Babe was an avid hunter and much better at hunting than barbering, duck hunting being his speciality. Early one morning he arrived at the duck blind, reached into the trunk of his car, pulled the loaded shotgun out, tripping the trigger and killing himself instantly. Babe's had been the place where all the big shots in city government had their hair cut, and was also used by all the locals as a betting parlor. That one incident seem to set off a murmur of the events of things to come, none of them good. The barber shop closing was ill luck as it had been part of our neighborhood for years. But bringing in a mission directly across the street from the barber shop gave everyone an uneasy feeling.

Union Mission, a rather fancy name for a run down building, had blossomed over the last year with Reverend Stroud as the director and preacher. He was a slim little man, with long hair parted in the middle that fell to his collar, and a deep bass voice which echoed through the little chapel as he gave his sermon to the attending street people who felt it a small price to pay for a decent meal. Stroud wore second hand suits, had an accent which was half hillbilly and half Okie. But through salesmanship and a pious manner received large donations from churches all over the city .To the local down-and-outers the mission was a disgrace to the neighborhood. One could hear them say, "God damn it, that place is bringing in so many bums they're going to run us out of our home." The guys who worked at the shop and the shop owners seemed to agree. Our street people were not as clean, and most of the time had far too much to drink. Through my plate glass window I would often see them trying to dodge the two telephone poles outside. They would side step one and walk directly into the other. But they were kind to each other and more courteous, not like the new guys who were younger and had a nasty, almost superior atmosphere about them. One felt that the new bums would like nothing better than a chance to kick hell out of the regulars.

Babe's and the mission were two blocks away and there was only a small murmur along the street until Abie died. With Chlem Sheet Metal directly across the street from the shop, the crumbling effect of the area became more apparent. The energy, the vitality that he brought to the street seemed to make the people lose their grip. Abie's death saddened Dad much more than he expected or admitted. One could see Abie running across Poplar almost every day, his little legs churning, his bald head shining, just to tell a dirty joke, or let Dad in on some shenanigans that a city official had pulled, usually ones that would never make the papers. Then there was Christmas time when the street in front of his shop was lined with uniformed policemen waiting their turn to receive a free fifth of whisky, a small gratuity for owning a liquor store. More than once Dad would call Abie late at night to get one of our men out of jail, something Abie never mentioned, only glancing into the shop to be sure the man was free. When I estimated a job for him on the sly, though I'm sure Dad knew, Abie would slip me a twenty, which I would refuse even as I was reaching for the money. Abie's life lived on in the stories that were told about him in the years to come, some exaggerated, but most true.

Mr. Crow still had his shoe shop, continued to get drunk each day and curse the United States, still went to Court Square on Sunday to preach Communism. There may be haggling with one of the local whores, but certainly not as homely as Mrs. Crow who had died of one of the many maladies that she had contracted over the years. Sam's Grocery had closed and he could now fish every day. No one knew what his wife would do with her spare time now that Abie was gone. Mrs. Mary kept her café open, still always neat as a pin and somehow surviving. Birmingham, who I could still remember being slapped by Cal, was more slovenly and seemed to get drunk more quickly as he sat at the back table drinking beer and telling dirty jokes to a younger, more hip bunch who didn't laugh quite as easily.

Things really began to unravel when the prostitutes from the apartment building across the street began to leave. The high steppers had gradually moved from Poplar to the Green Beetle at Vance and Main. It was the same bar that me and my mates had gone to just a few years before to drink sloe gin, throw up, and get into fights. It had now become the hangout for college boys and the girls who had left the nest on Poplar took up their positions on bar stools at the Beetle. There, they could pick and choose over a clientele that had a lot more money, and where they had the convenience of Frank's pay-by-the-hour hotel just across the street. The Green Beetle, the high-steppers, and Frank's Hotel all flourished, as did Jimmy's the liquor store on the corner, who still kept a large supply of sloe gin.

The mothers who had seen their young fly the coop still had skid row, but the pickings were slim. Soon these ladies, who considered themselves mature rather than aged, left the place they had called home, where their mothers had been prostitutes before them, and moved to a honky-tonk across from the train station. Hazel's Café sat the corner of Main and Calhoun, was painted a more putrid color than Dad's office, had darkened windows, and a door that had a large poorly scripted notice on it stating, "No loitering allowed." The place was a wino's dream, as dark as night even on the brightest of days, and was furnished with stools where the mature women who had now become street whores could slouch and have a much better chance of being picked up. The Green Beetle was only two blocks away, but to these ladies who were competing with their own daughters it was a lifetime. Before long they would be forced outside to stand on the corner next to the ladies of a much darker color who were a lot less prissy and much more open about what hey had to offer. In the end these once promising women faded into the background, probably to the farms in outlying areas from where their mothers had started their journey years before.

With the death of Abie and the flight of the prostitutes, things continued to unravel. On a bright, sunshiny day in May a short, extremely plump man, dressed in an ill fitting black suit, complete with black tie, and a dark hat pulled far down on his forehead looking very much like the local undertaker, came into the office. It was warm enough for the floor fan to be on, but the cool look of the black suited man made Dad frown. The gentleman, speaking in a high pitched voice and somewhat condescending manner, stated that he was from the Engineering Office and that the city had decided to demolish the neighborhood…to demolish the place that the name Werner had been associated with since 1900. The city fathers and the public in general had long considered the area a disgrace, so while widening Lauderdale Avenue and cutting it through to Jackson Avenue there was a legitimate excuse to tear down all the old buildings. Dad wouldn't talk to the man, deciding that I should be the spokesman and pointed at me, saying, "Talk to him JoJo." Hell, I didn't know what to say either. Dad was furious, I was confused, and the chap who had come in with the happy news that we would soon be out of this dump was beginning to frown ."Don't you understand?" he asked, looking around at the fake paneling in my office. "We're going to pay you to move to another location and build a new building." Things quickly took a turn for the worse. Dad did some of the best yelling he had done since Louis was around, and the city man left muttering something about Imminent Domain forcing us out.

Dad was becoming more and more bitter. The characters were fading away. Guys who could never be trusted to show up on Monday morning, who might get drunk on the job, whose first stop each day was a liquor store were disappearing. They were the ones I had known since I was a child. If there was trouble on a job, as was often the case because of my poor estimating, they would somehow pull my butt out of a crack. They were full of life but for the most part died young. In quick succession, Gurley died of a ruined liver, and Hank was hospitalized with venereal disease. Do Right, unlike his name, just wouldn't, and after I had to get him off of a five story building when drunk, Dad fired him. He died as a drunk on the streets. Grinder had ruined his feet in a fall, and Chester was testing out the Chicago jails. Joe Phelps and Junior had taken the same route by putting guns to their heads. For Junior it was because the country boy had been caught up in the city and become a drug addict. For Joe, because his wife ran off with another man. Bevo's arthritis had finally gotten the best of him, but he was still a champ in my book. Thank God good guys like Pear, Cal and Charley were still hanging in there, working just as hard as ever.

The man from the city kept coming around, and gradually it sunk in that we were going to have to relocate. While I figured the dreaded duct jobs, Dad would get in the car and drive in ever widening circles to find a new location for the shop, but like a wayward child afraid to wander too far from home. With help from Tom, the fellow from the city, who had become friends with Dad one afternoon when he pulled off his tie and offered to buy us all a beer, Dad located a lot to build on only a few blocks from Poplar, on Court St. This pleased Dad to no end since the house on Jones St. ,the old shop, and the location for the new shop were within rock throwing distance of each other.

Within a month we had a contractor to build a new and better shop with bigger offices, and I had landed two really nice sized duct jobs. We sat in the old office and the four of us drank a beer one afternoon. I had to fetch the beer from Mrs. Mary since she still didn't believe Louie was twenty one. My chest filled with sorrow as I recalled the time Louie and I had painted the concrete block office that awful lime green color my sister the artist had selected, and the memory of those old-timers whose ghosts we were leaving behind. I didn't want to leave the sight of those scratch marks from Louis's matches, or the box with the coldest beer in town, and it made me sad to see the defeated look on my Dad's face. We were going on to better things. But sitting there with the only light coming from the gooseneck lamp, I knew that from time on it would be Dad in the background. I felt an awful lump in my throat. We were stepping over a new threshold, taking a direction in life that was far different from our ways on skid row.

26

DREAMS REALLY DO COME TRUE

Amelia and I were like all young people when we were first married; we lived on dreams, love, and faith, disappointment never entered the equation. We had no doubt that we would have children. But by the time Amelia became pregnant for the fifth time, I had surely come down to earth. My dreams were a thing of the past, my faith was a question mark, but my love for my wife and son were stronger than ever. I was sick and worried about Steve as he watched his mother go through those traumas each year. As Catholics we used no artificial preventative. Instead we used something called the rhythm system, a practice the Catholic Church endorsed and the nuns and priests had insisted we practice. It very simply meant that we not make love on certain days of the month.

We argued about her becoming pregnant again. Arguing in our house was me yelling and Amelia never saying a word. But at times she could be more bull headed than me. When I came home one afternoon and she was leaning against the post on our front porch, legs crossed, holding Steve on her hip and grinning like a possum I knew that once again she was pregnant, but for the first time there was promise.

Some months before our friend Dr. Arnoult had called and asked that we meet him in his office one Saturday morning. He was gracious and kind as usual and I had the same feeling as always, almost as if we were his children. He started out by saying, "Now look, I don't want you to get your hopes up, but I've been in contact with an agency of the government who is experimenting with a new drug." He further explained directly to Amelia, who after all was to be the guinea pig, "The drug must be administered by shot each week for one month. Our hope is that the drug will act as a barrier for the antibodies being produced by your blood, a dam so to speak, which will prevent the red cells being destroyed in the unborn infant." He added, again more to Amelia than me, "We must face the fact that in your fifth pregnancy these antibodies have become so strong the chances are slim, even with the new drug."

The doctor, who had become more our friend and ally, had already gotten approval, not wanting to disappoint us if he failed, but repeated that this was only an experiment. We talked for hours, his usually tense face relaxed. He asked us to lunch, almost as if he didn't want to leave us, not wanting to lose sight of Amelia's beaming smile. At lunch Dr. Arnoult told us the cost of these shots, a total of twelve, and as usual my stomach started hurting, taking my appetite away. We still owed for the last baby, hospitals and doctors, including Dr. Arnoult. The bills just seemed to keep piling up, and the doctor grinned and said, "Don't worry about it Joe, there will be no charge for these shots since they're experimental." We left Dr. Arnoult feeling better than we had in years. It was one of those special days, the kind that we had so few of in the last years. We went to Mom's and ate again, then picked up Steve and went to the Zoo where the three of us became silly, riding the merry-go-round and eating too much cotton candy. Then we walked to the little arbor where Amelia and I sat on Sunday afternoons just a few years before. It was one of those magical afternoons when time moved as slowly as dew drying on a leaf. I held Steve in my lap and he seemed to be perfectly content, finally going to sleep in my arms while the two of us talked in whispers as the breeze blew through Amelia's hair, reminding me of the young girl I had known as a teenager. We had come a long way in such a short while, and with each step we loved each other more, our problems had only made us grow closer.

Amelia was six months pregnant and proudly showing off her round stomach which seemed to grow every day, and I was trying to figure out how we were going to fit a new baby in an already crowded apartment. We had found a lot in an area named Prospect Park and had managed a down payment on it, but we would never be able to raise the money to start a house before the baby was born.

With a new shop about to be built and more work to figure than we could take care of, the Werner name was being used on more and more projects. With the union having settled into a dog fight every four years when a new contract was to be signed, a certain calm existed on the surface but underneath things were ready to boil at any moment. Since the Korean war had ended new plants and schools were needed, causing a terrific boom in construction and Dad was starting to smile again. Finding a place to build a new shop in the same area as the one on Poplar made him feel more secure.

Amelia began taking the shots each week which were terribly painful, being administered into each cheek of her buttocks. She would come out of the hospital quoting Mom, " It just gets my goat that those nurses can never stick the needle where it won't hurt." But pain or not, her face had a healthy glow. With each passing day the baby was moving, something which fascinated Steve as he watched for hours, then laid his head against her stomach to listen to the baby's heartbeat.

It was a Sunday morning, which meant the three of us would lay in bed together and talk before dressing for church, when the telephone rang. It was the nurse for Dr. Davis, who said "Please meet the doctor at St. Joseph as soon as possible." Dr. Davis, the Pathologist who was in charge of monitoring the drug was one of those unfortunate people who had the appearance and demeanor of someone our bunch had picked on when we were kids. He was young but being almost bald and slump shouldered gave one the feeling of middle age. He was also extremely serious and unknowingly sarcastic. No matter how hard we tried, we just couldn't like him.

I packed Amelia into the old Ford and again left a frightened Steve with Caroline, then rushed to the hospital. When we walked into the room we were met by the grim faces of Dr. Arnoult and Dr. Davis. In a slow southern drawl, speaking so softly that we could hardly understand him Dr. Davis said, "I'm sorry to tell you this, but the drug you are taking doesn't work, there is even the possibility that it might be harmful." Dr. Arnoult was silent, his face closed in, and when I looked at Amelia I saw for the first time on her tear stained face a look of defeat. I began in silence to cuss God and the son-of-a-bitch who invented this so called miracle drug, the priests and nuns who never showed up to offer us solace, only the wrath of God, and myself for letting this charade go so far. If I loved my wife so much, I thought, why hadn't I told the doctors to tie her tubes after all those dead babies? Why had I listened to the Church and its teachings? And why did I think our love and Amelia's simple trust could bring us a healthy baby?

After a silence that lasted far too long, Dr. Davis turned to Dr. Arnoult, "We've come so far," he said, "Even though the drug didn't work the baby is obviously alive and active." Again, addressing Dr. Arnoult he said, "Could we not check Amelia every week for red blood cell count? She's already six months pregnant and if the antibodies begin building too rapidly we can take the baby by a caesarian operation , then change the newborn's blood." Dr. Arnoult who had been silent during the entire discussion turned, " What do the two of you say? Don't you think it's worth a chance?"

With that the meeting was over and Amelia and I left, neither of us convinced that anything good was going to happen. If the antibodies were building up with each pregnancy we were sure that before long her stomach would quit growing and the baby would quit moving.

Time moved like the proverbial snail. Amelia kept growing and the baby was as active as ever. I came home from work, hugged Steve so hard it hurt, then the two of us leaned our heads against Amelia's stomach and listened to the heartbeat of our child, strong as a church bell. The three of us began to smile again. Steve had become part of our conspiracy. We were going to beat the odds, the antibodies became our enemy, the red cells our friends. We had no weapons to win this battle but pure stubborn faith and a young woman who would never, never, give up. Work became more tedious with each day, waiting for the next time when I could take Amelia to the hospital for her check-up, holding our breath while we waited for the results, praying that the red blood cell count had not dropped. Everyone wanted to help, and when Dr. Davis mentioned that the baby would need the blood to be replaced all the men at the shop, all our friends, and all the family, rushed to donate, happy to at least feel as if they were part of something special. And as the time grew nearer and the red cells held their own, our family and friends, and people we hardly knew, wanted to help.

There was still work to be done. On a morning in November I took the truck and delivered some material to a small tedious job we were doing, then stayed to help the men finish up. We cleaned up and returned to the shop and as I got within a block I could see Mom standing in the doorway frantically waving her arms. Of course the two guys knew what was happening and jumped off the truck, and before I could utter a word Mom had jumped on the running board and climbed into the cab, all four feet ten of her. "JoJo, Amelia's red blood count dropped badly and they are going to operate right now." We tore off to St. Joseph. I hardly remembered driving or parking or being too impatient to wait on the elevator, instead running up the four flights of stairs only to find that we were too late, and Amelia had already been taken to the operating room. Only then did I realize that my mother had chased up the stairs after me and was now paying the price for it. The bad heart that she had suffered with for years must have been giving her hell. She was gray faced and shaking like a leaf. A floor nurse ran to the front desk and brought her a heart pill while I laid her in a chair and put a wet cloth on her forehead, then sat next to her and waited.

Aunt Ruth came running down the hall, having already looked in the operating room. She had a smile that lit up the entire floor, calling out "JoJo, Amelia's doing great, they are going to take the baby right away," and with that turned and raced back to the operating room. What seemed like hours, but was probably only a few minutes, passed. Then the operating room door burst open and Dr. Arnoult dashed down the hall, coat tail flying, and a panicky expression on his face with a small bundle in his arms. Within an hour the family began to arrive, all talking at once, filling the room with chatter, everyone waiting for our messenger. When Ruth arrived she opened the doors in her white suit and cap set to perfection, she curtsied, something she had probably never done in her life, and with a glowing smile said, "Joe, you have a healthy wife and a beautiful baby girl." She told us that Dr. Arnoult had changed the baby's blood and that the baby had screamed during the entire procedure. We all waited and soon Dr. Arnoult came out in a bloody apron, a worried expression on his face, calling me aside saying, "Joe, I'm afraid the

first transfusion hasn't done the job, we're going to have to try again."
Without another word he was gone. Everyone sat and fretted, our only
link being Ruth. She flitted from the recovery room where Amelia
lay, to the operating room down the hall, checking on mother and
child then reporting back with that wonderful smile of hers in place
even as the worry showed through. Finally Dr. Arnoult emerged from
the operating room, ignored everyone but me and solemnly grabbed
my hand with both of his and shook it saying, " Joe, you have a fine
healthy girl. The second transfusion did the job. You have no need to
worry." With that he stood patiently and talked to the family, looking
terribly exhausted but with a look of satisfaction.

Soon it seemed that the entire hospital had heard about our baby.
The waiting room and hallway were packed with onlookers pushing
aside our family, everyone asking, some demanding, to see what
the hospital priest called the "Miracle Baby." It was the same priest
who never came to see Amelia when she needed someone to offer her
comfort. The head nun, who always stayed at the end of the hall not
wanting to see Amelia when she lost another child, crowded in with
the others whispering about the miracle child. The whole scene was
almost out of control until the Werners and Solari's literally pushed
everyone out of the area.

Late that night when some semblance of peace was restored

and I had finally seen a beautiful baby who would be named Ruth, I held that precious bundle close to my heart and laid her down next to her mother with her freshly scrubbed face and radiant smile. I picked up my son, who had been sound asleep in the chair. As I stood in my dirty clothes I said to myself, "For some, what we saw happen today will seem like a miracle. But to me this baby was born because a young girl had the grit and determination to believe, and because of the pure, sweet, love of two young people."

EPILOGUE

There the story should end, but not quite. The few months that Amelia and I had with Steve and Ruth were the happiest of our marriage until the unthinkable happened. Amelia was pregnant again. We were certain by now that Ruth would be our last child. Amelia had been through enough. All the doctors had agreed that her body would not produce another baby that would live. Yet somehow in my carelessness she had become pregnant again. Ruth was just a few months old, yet all our happiness was washed away in our simple act of love.

We were again taking that drive we knew so well to the doctor's office when Amelia burst out crying." I'm so damn tired of being pregnant," she sobbed, "It just doesn't seem fair." I sat like a fool, holding the steering wheel tight, saying nothing, knowing I had no answer.

When we arrived we were ushered directly into the doctor's office, where he sat, his round little belly lapping over his belt. The usual arrogance was gone, replaced by a weariness I had never seen before. Without preamble he said, "I'm sorry, your wife is three months pregnant, and the baby is already dead." Without touching my wife, which would surely have turned loose our pent up emotions, I asked "What can we do now, what is the next step?" The doctor said, "Amelia will have to carry the baby for a short while longer, then we can take the infant by caesarian section." And before I could ask more, he said "Joe, you do realize that you are putting your wife in danger every time she gets pregnant. I strongly suggest that Amelia should have her tubes tied." I looked at Amelia and she gazed at the floor, not meeting my eyes. I wanted to reach for her, to hold her, but kept my distance, and said, "How soon can it be done?"

We left at once and drove home. As we did I thought of the misery that Amelia had suffered because we played by the rules of the Catholic Church. Amelia had always left it up to me and I wanted to tell her, and I would in time, that any shame would be mine alone. Now we were going to be done with it, and we felt no guilt.

The month went quickly. When it was time I took her to Methodist Hospital to have the dead infant. St. Joseph Hospital had refused to admit her because her tubes were to be tied. The hospital was rigid in its refusal, as if to say, "We will allow you to bring her to have a dead baby, and another, and another until she dies, but don't come if you want to save her life." Amelia had the child and the doctor tied her tubes.

When Amelia had recovered there was a stillness about her. If we went to church she would never go to communion. When I asked she said, "I feel like an outcast. I just don't feel right going to communion." With that I decided to take the only step that I knew would ease her pain.

Saint Paul Catholic Church was in Whitehaven, a suburb of Memphis, and the pastor was a middle aged priest with a fiery temper, and definite views. I called and asked if Amelia and I could meet with him. On a sunny afternoon in May, one of those days that Memphis has so many of in late spring, the three of us sat in his rectory. The sun shone though the windows high in the wall, giving the whole room a feeling of serenity, and a sense of peace settled over the two of us. The priest was a surprisingly easy man to talk to; quiet when he needed to be, listening for the longest time as I explained all that had happened in the last six years. When I finished what amounted to a confession, the priest sighed. Then he sat back and closed his eyes. After a few minutes he looked at the two of us, then turned to Amelia and said, "I don't how you suffered through it." He stood and said, "Come on with me and let's get this nonsense out of the way. We'll make it official." We followed him into the church to the confessional. There, one by one, we repeated our conversation from the rectory. Our sins had been absolved by that simple act, sins in word only, for we felt no guilt.

Many, many years have passed. Skid row has vanished, gone in the name of progress. "Depression" became a word for history books.

The tinners I had known as a young man exist now only in the stories I tell. They were the guys who might never show up on Monday, they were uneducated, and sometimes made foolish mistakes, but they had compassion and loyalty. I tell my grandchildren about my teenage years, when I stopped for the men to get a pint on the way to a job, or the parade when all the men got drunk, and the sense of freedom I felt when I sat on a scaffold board at the top of a steeple. We were the rounders, the guys who worked for *Werner Sheet Metal* and we were proud of it.

Amelia and I were just kids when it all started. We had nothing but dreams, and each other. Then our world grew. We had our son and our daughter. Ruth would never be affected by her transfusions. She would become a beautiful young lady, marry a sturdy young man , and have two daughters of her own. Steve would grow and become a fine, gentle husband, and the father of two wonderful sons. And Amelia and I would grow old together and I would look at her and still see that cute young girl with legs a little too thin, wearing loafers with white bobby socks. There would be many bumps along the way, some little, and some awfully big, but with every day our love would grow. So you see, dreams really do come true.

ABOUT THE AUTHOR

Joe Werner is a retired contractor.

He and his wife Amelia live in Memphis; they travel much of the year, both in the states and overseas.

Printed in the United States
64140LVS00004B/334-408

9 781420 894561